First published in Great Britain in 2000 by
Wiley-Academy. A division of John Wiley & Sons, Baffins Lane, Chichester, West Sussex, PO19 1UD.
ISBN: 0-471-623636

Other Wiley Editorial Offices: New York, Weinheim, Brisbane, Singapore, Toronto.
Design & Art Direction: Alun Evans & Katy Hepburn.
Printed and bound in Italy.

ACKNOWLEDGEMENTS

Every book has its legacy and debt of gratitude - this is no less true in this case.

In the very first instance, I owe it to Richard Meier and his work, which has brought me to New York on a regular basis since 1993. Next, to Professor Kenneth Frampton who first introduced me to Thomas Hanrahan and Victoria Meyers, and recommended their excellent work. A subsequent visit to their superb Holley Loft, and a discussion with their client, not only confirmed Frampton's recommendation, but also founded the idea for this book.

Following that first and crucial encounter, I owe a great gratitude to Victoria Meyers, in particular – for she then introduced me to the other nine architects whose work forms the substance of this review, together with that of Hanrahan and Meyers.

I am especially grateful to all the architects and their staff, and of course to their clients, for allowing access to their private domain during the subsequent research and site visits in New York itself. Equally, I am grateful for all the visual and drawn material each designer has made available to us for publication.

I cannot write this note without also thanking all the photographers involved for all their excellent work, without which no proper publication would be possible.

On the same basis, I extend my thanks to Victoria Meyers for her unfailing advice and help throughout, and to her and Richard Gluckman and his architects, for the same in the closing stages of this publication.

Finally, I would particularly like to thank Maggie Toy and all the staff of Wiley/Academy in London, including Abigail Grater and Mariangela Palazzi-Williams, and the book designers Alun Evans and Katy Hepburn, for their complete support in bringing this publication to realisation.

Ivor Richards
For Sarah and Owen

Front cover: interior view of the Holley Loft by Thomas Hanrahan & Victoria Meyers (Photo © Peter Aaron/Esto)
Back cover: interior view of the New York Apartment by Frank Lupo & Daniel Rowen (Photo © Michael Moran)

manhattan lofts

IVOR RICHARDS

Quandt Loft: major reception space

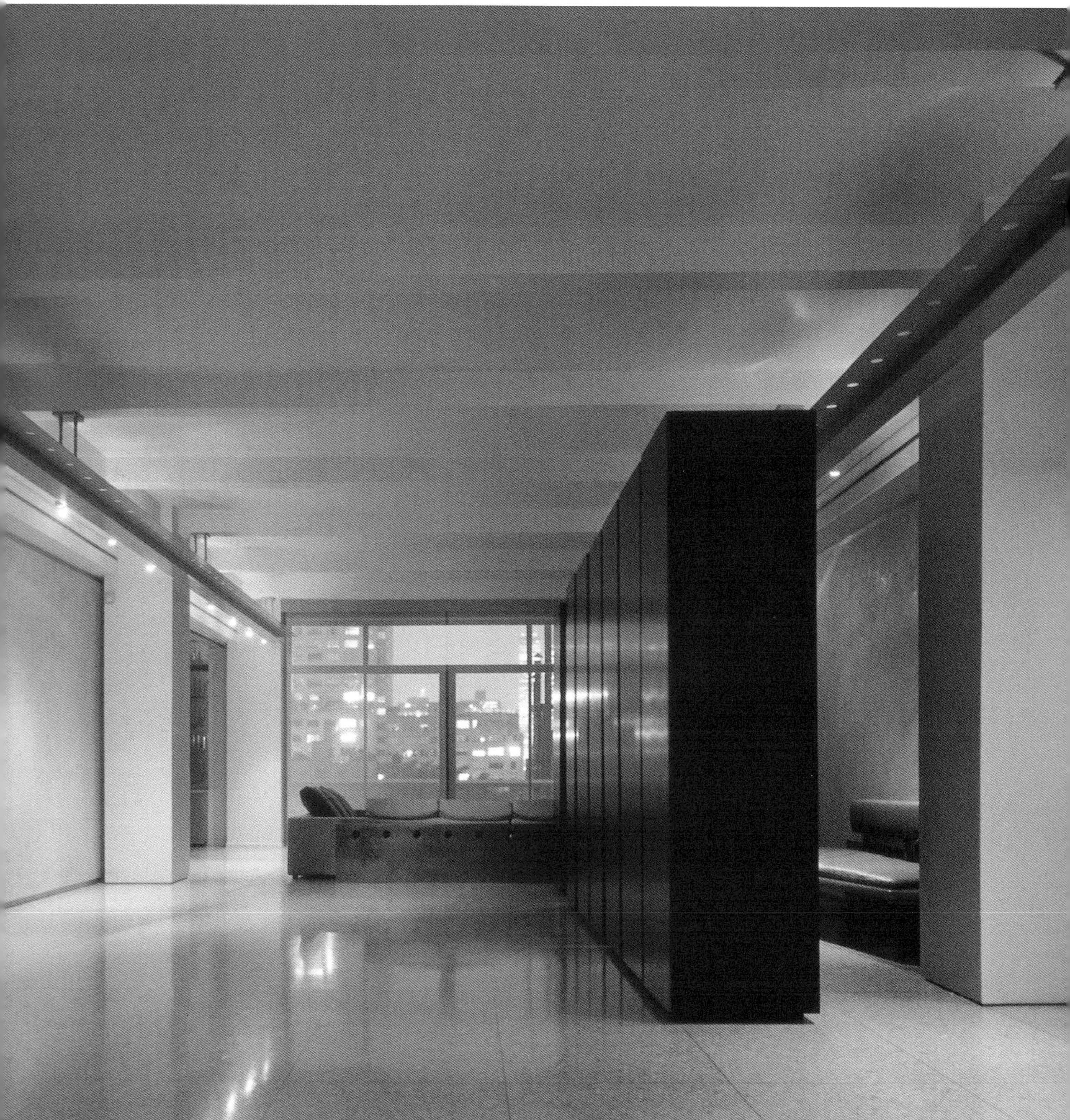

The New York City loft has become a tradition. At this point, in 1999, it is possible to look back at the evolution of the loft as an architectural type, its lineage and influence being of such strength that the traditional apartment in itself has been transcended by the nature of the loft, in particular by the general nature of its spatiality.

It is well understood in New York, especially in Soho and Tribeca and other related areas where this study is based, that as factories and other industrial uses moved out in the late 1950s, so the conversion and refurbishment that followed provided for a whole new generation of loft dwellers, occupying the generous space that had once formed the cramped conditions, a generation earlier, for large numbers of industrial workers.

Large areas of the urban city-blocks near to harbor and shipping facilities contain huge ranges of warehousing used originally to store commodities and foodstuffs. These buildings, with innovative design transformation, form the basis for the archetypal Manhattan Loft, where in Soho, for instance, a population of artists first established the New York tradition of the urban atelier. The high floor to ceiling dimensions, typically 12 feet, often coupled with good end or side-lighting from day-lit windows, stood in the tradition of the European artist's atelier, although not all the sites within any given warehouse or similar structure offer the ideal balance of daylight, space, and views.

Quandt Loft: living area
Next page: Holley Loft: view towards
colonnaded music gallery & foyer

A typical loft condition could yield a cross-wall structure with a clear internal dimension of at least 24 feet and might be mixed with intermediate cast-iron columns with a heavy floor structure of close-centered timber beams, whose structural capacity determined the basic spans and internal dimensions limited by the industrial uses and resultant loadings. While the variety of structural types varies from large open frames of columns and beams to smaller cross-wall cases, in essence the starting point is an open universal space, with heavy industrial standard services.

It is not the central purpose of this deliberately limited survey to present a history of the evolution of the loft. This has been, in any case, thoroughly presented in earlier publications,[1] where there has also been an intention to demonstrate the almost boundless succession of designer intervention and interior-decor options, framed under a series of headings, after the manner of interior journals and magazines, dealing with the modern home. Equally, there have been monographic works dedicated to the output of certain designers whose contribution to the evolution of the loft as sites for the craft of interior design, has an established reputation and recent history.[2]

The purpose of this current survey is to present a critical view of the Manhattan Loft as a definitive architectural typology whose central discipline lies in the mutation of pure space and materiality, as realized in the architectural landscape of the interior, whose common theme is openness. And this critical assemblage is intended to reveal, as a function of the contemporary condition in New York architecture, the product of an emergent generation of architects and clients. It also collectively evidences the nature of a developing modernity, based on a flexible spatiality, which is not about fashion but a deeper sense of rooted settlement and the restorative values of ordered space and light within the basic structure of a personal retreat. The examples presented are, at first sight, all very different, some are Minimalist – others more opulent and sophisticated. What is common throughout the twelve sites considered is that these are all works of architecture, conceived within the pluralistic framework of the modern project as a whole. These architectural works are then considered in detail, and the critical review is set within the context of the whole group of ten architects who have generously revealed and showcased their exemplary work, for the purposes of this presentation. In certain cases, the architects' own notes are included.

New York Apartment: interior view

TWELVE PROJECTS – TEN ARCHITECTS

It is recognized, in the first instance, that any selective survey cannot possibly represent all the varieties of architectural position, nor the diversities of requirements and personal tastes of the extraordinary range and status of clients for the Manhattan loft or apartment. However, the collection set out in this critique displays a representative richness, even taking account of the deliberate and rigorous nature of our selection from a self-evidently broad area of architectural activity, that is current in Manhattan, or drawn from the last decade of architects' works.[3]

The twelve projects and their architects that form the basis for this general critical overview, in architectural sets, are as follows:

HOLLEY LOFT
Hanrahan & Meyers

MoMA TOWER APARTMENT
Hanrahan & Meyers

NEW YORK APARTMENT
Lupo & Rowen

17TH STREET LOFT
Bernard Tschumi

ROSENFELD LOFT
Richard Gluckman

BOESKY LOFT
Richard Gluckman

MOSS LOFT
Smith-Miller & Hawkinson

QUANDT LOFT
Williams & Tsien

SCHNEIDER PENTHOUSE
Hariri & Hariri

CHELSEA LOFT
Marble & Fairbanks

O/K APARTMENT
Kolatan & MacDonald

'K' LOFT
George Ranalli

The first architectural set of lofts are, in their physical reality, both various in the materiality of their presence and in date. The common aspiration in each lies in an absolute commitment to the space of modernity – open and flowing, an endless becoming – and a rigorous Minimalism[4] that offers many internal vistas, planar elements instead of walls and a definitive, Spartan strictness in the arrangement of material elements and their fabric, which exploits limitation. This communality has arisen quite naturally and it is particularly reassuring to find such a coherent extension of the modern project, offered casually, without rhetoric and with all the richness of contextual variety that genuine modern architecture has consistently been able to yield, in its response to program, place, and clientele.

There is, evidently, a very close relationship in architectural format and spatial enclosure between the Holley Loft (Hanrahan & Meyers) and the rare and spectacular New York Apartment (Lupo & Rowen). When first crossing the threshold of these projects, the overwhelming impression is of the spiritual elevation that is carried in the quality and generosity of the free-plan and its responsive, calm, open, and fluid spatiality. The common framework, without reservation, is the adoption of a planar discipline – the legacy of Mies van der Rohe – which, in each case, reverses the kind of parti of the Barcelona Pavilion, and contains all spatial areas within a boundless edge, which in the instance of the New York Apartment is dissolved in light.

While the Holley Loft is rich and golden in its aura with natural materials in evidence that connect with the outer world, the New York Apartment project is hierarchically neutral[5] and achieves an almost sublime condition of peaceful, spatial sanctuary. In both cases, walls as elements of storage or program, such as library or office, subsume the concept of rooms. Equally, both are dwelling places that are idealized and designed around the lifestyle of one or two individuals with specific residential requirements, in contrast to some other lofts in this series, which are for families with children.

Holley Loft: dining space seen from entrance

The Museum of Modern Art (MoMA) Tower Apartment (Hanrahan & Meyers) presents a reverse spatial condition to that of the Holley Loft, but it is detailed with an equally intense precision. In order to maximize the sense of a spatial scale within the confines of the two-room apartment, the architects have developed a language of what they describe as 'swift and slow space' – a dialog of movement between active-reflective and inactive-matte surfaces, within the cubic interior volume. Regardless of scale, therefore, the essential communality of the Holley Loft and the MoMA Apartment resides in the realm of extended spatiality, and a rich materiality of surface, detail, and installations – each a highly personalized, interior architectural domain.

The Tschumi loft shares many of the characteristics of the Holley Loft and the New York Apartment, but is a singular simple statement, delivered in black and white with a clear line between public and private space, and with some flexibility on that crucial boundary.

17th Street Loft

Richard Gluckman has established his position as an architect who is a renowned master of reductive, sparse materiality and restrained intervention. Gluckman's architectural language is particularly appropriate to the settings for Minimalist art that he is famed for housing, in many gallery buildings.

Alongside the major commissions for the arts, over the recent years, Gluckman has also produced a series of singular and significant projects for lofts in Manhattan. Among these, the Rosenfeld Loft (1999) is an archetypal exemplar of Gluckman's work, which incorporates the restraint of an absolute Minimalist intervention to the existing fabric, juxtaposed with a tightly orchestrated set of sophisticated inserts, within the interior shell. The magnificent sobriety of Gluckman's white architectural domain and major spaces is therefore pierced and occupied by material events related to specific functions.

The Boesky residence (1999), a parallel Gluckman project, is distinguished by a two-storey volume and for the exhibition requirements of an art dealer. The project consists of a public lower floor, and a private upper floor with den, master bedroom, and a significant roof terrace. The white interior is juxtaposed against a dark, ebony-stained, riffcut wide plank oak floor, a theme Gluckman has included in earlier loft projects. The two levels are functionally divided by inserted elements, such as kitchen enclosure or a 'thick' fireplace wall. The life of the occupants is enhanced by the introduction of natural top light, and the extension of the private upper-level space on to the unexpectedly large roof-terrace, which is half the length of the whole linear plan-form.

1	LIVING
2	DINING
3	KITCHEN
4	GALLERY
5	ENTRY
6	STUDY
7	GUEST ROOM
8	BATHROOM
9	PANTRY
10	TERRACE
11	STUDY
12	BEDROOM
13	BATHROOM
14	LAUNDRY
15	CLOSET

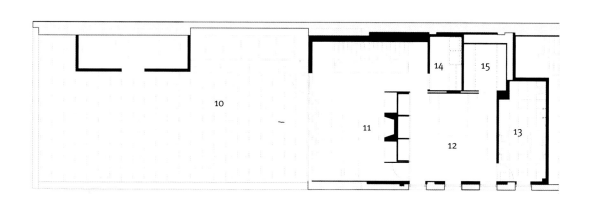

BOESKY LOFT / PLANS

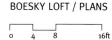

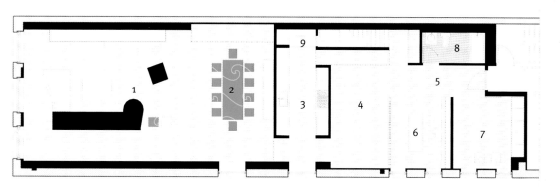

Boesky Loft

The seventh project of the set is the work of Henry Smith-Miller and Laurie Hawkinson, the Moss Loft, New York (1990). The project is characterized by the interpretation of the program for a fashion designer's studio and residence. The design is essentially part of a set of projects including a Model Apartment and a Penthouse Apartment (1993), and the Rotunda Gallery, also a loft conversion of the same year (1989). All these projects maximize and accentuate the quality and openness of interior space, modulated by inserts, fittings and the use of huge, pivotal or sliding door-wall elements. The material nature and highest standards of construction and finish, together with an inherent flexibility and controlled lightness of presence, underpin a range of work that is an absolutely exemplary and uncompromising extension of architecture in modernity.

The assembled work of Hanrahan & Meyers, Lupo & Rowen, Tschumi, Gluckman and Smith-Miller & Hawkinson brings together the finest evidence of a new school of architecture, in New York, that has recently embraced the principles of the modern project and yet advanced these within a strict spatial–material discipline, almost endless in its variation and response to clientele and place.

These are small works but, at the same time, *real* works of architecture.

Moss Loft: detail of steel sliding & pivot doors

Model Apartment New York: 'urban dwelling apparatus'

Opposite page: New York Penthouse Apartment: open living space, western view
Below: Rotunda Gallery: Brooklyn 1993. Gallery seen from bridge / detail

The second architectural set of Lofts are characterised by their scale and their reflection of the sophisticated, luxurious quality that is possible given a certain type of clientele and architects of particular capacity for elegant elaboration. Albeit, these works are equally faithful to the essentials of a developing tradition in modern architecture and have a restrained allegiance to various strands of that legacy, from the 1920s to the present day.

Perhaps the most magnificent project of this whole selection, is the Quandt Loft, by Tod Williams and Billie Tsien, with David van Handel. It is, like the New York Apartment (Lupo and Rowen), essentially a masterpiece but in every sense, also, completely opposite and opulent. From the overall idea of the spatial format to the detail, the project reveals a masterly control of the making of place, form and exquisite detail and materiality, and function. Above all, it is the quiet maturity of the whole architecture of this place that is both monumental, impressive and yet comfortable and receptive. The *Quandt Loft* is a huge and yet memorable home, with specific areas capable of supporting a marvellous range of atmospheres and experiences of living, private work and retreat, and spiritual renewal and relaxation.

The Schneider Penthouse (1986) by Gisue and Mojgan Hariri, is equally special in its particular sense of place and detail and the controlled luxury of its format and accents. It contains their famous chef d'oeuvre, a hybrid stair part straight-flight, part spiral that is captured into a curving logarithmic spiral of (by now) weathered steel-sheet. This is all in the service of a duplex-space, the only loft on a two-floor section in this set, and complete with a beautiful and unexpected pergola-topped roof terrace, from the upper master bedroom level.

What is extremely rare and particular about the Hariri sisters' beautiful work is their sense of ancient craft, and the depth of recall and history this naturally implies. It is possibly something to do with their spendidly evidenced Persian inheritance that has confronted other traditions such as that of Eileen Gray, or Pierre Chareau, and the planar striations of Frank Lloyd Wright.

There is also a sensitivity to their client's sense of taste and colour that is carefully developed into a series of themes that reveal a kind of luxury, that is at the same time, both ordered and modest.

Schneider Penthouse:
stair detail

Quandt Loft: balcony detail

In contrast, the 5,000 square foot Chelsea Loft (1994-6) by Scott Marble and Karen Fairbanks – two of New York's '40 under 40' architectural talent grouping, is an essentially linear proposition, for a family with two children. An architectural interior, whose extended length – dedicated to the 'public-space' of the family, – is accentuated by natural side-lighting from its southern face. The idea of natural light is further developed in the geometric 'slicing' of flexible sliding wall elements, that open or close the main living spaces from the deeper interior areas of kitchen, breakfast, and family gathering space. In a similar manner it is possible to adjust the relationship between studio and master bedroom with a triplicate group of pivotal, perforate screens – again, a modulation of the potential of daylight penetration, and a play between public and private zones, within a flexible framework of space.

Chelsea Loft: 'public space'

In this case the materiality is less opulent, but the overall intention is clearly driven by the transformation of modest materials into elements of complexity – as evidenced in the mobile screens – which in turn also presents an image of restrained richness, taken together with the beautiful furniture of the main spaces.

Finally, the work of Sulan Kolatan and William MacDonald, and that of George Ranalli complete the sets of projects in this collection.

Kolatan and MacDonald, in all their work – but especially in their recently completed O/K Apartment – represent an extremity of the most overtly experimental, avant-garde of contemporary New York modernity. The confident exploration of transformations, a kind of organic plasticity that, at first sight, recalls Alison and Peter Smithson's 'House of the Future' from the '60s, is largely the result of Kolatan and MacDonald's current use of computer modelling. This all comes together in their extraordinary O/K Apartment, where spaces and functions are fused and modeled in a series of 'plastic' events set within a (relatively) conventional container which is finished in a yellow-green plaster.

Left: O/K Loft: bedroom space
Opposite page: 'M' Loft: Kolatan & MacDonald. "...openness, transparency & reflectivity..."

George Ranalli, a scholar of Frank Lloyd Wright and his projects[6] and the work of Carlo Scarpa,[7] is also a teacher and practitioner who has devoted much of his effort to the development of an interior architecture.[8] His 'K' Loft is among the best of his works. In a standard loft dimension, in this case with superb cross-vaulting in brick, supported on brick cross-walls, he has created both open and contained spaces carved, spliced, and paneled in brick, plywood, plaster, glass, and maple – within the brick shell, that has formed a powerful and homely retreat for two artists and their child. Again, it is a project that is a product of two forces – the act of craft and the creation of space, for the enclosure of family life and work. Ranalli represents a respectful continuity of Wright and a reverence of Scarpa – and despite the intensely worked nature of his projects, there is a sense of inhabited warmth and welcome that endures, and carries with it the tradition of Frank Lloyd Wright in particular.

The parallels and contrasts in this series of projects are unavoidably diverse. They all evidence the continuing development of the process of modernity, and its endless response to program and place, within the modern project as a whole.

K Loft: main interior space

Loft projects in detail

Holley Loft

Thomas Hanrahan and Victoria Meyers

1995

The spirit of the design process, that is central to the work of Hanrahan and Meyers, is captured in their conceptual drawings and paintings. These include 'process collages,' concept and massing studies in isometric, and idealized, abstracted, elemental color paintings.

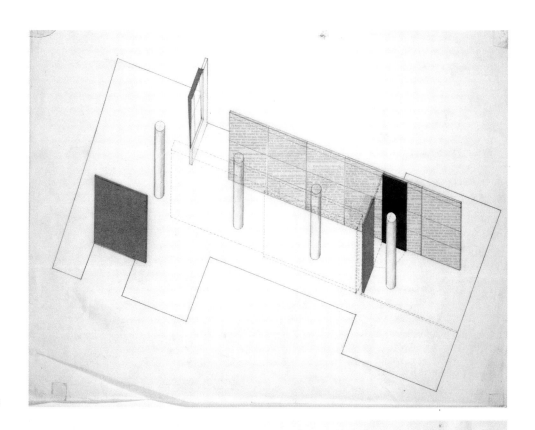

Holley Loft: conceptual studies

The composition of their architectural work involves a distinctly Miesian-planar method of assembling elements of function and enclosure. The spatial system is worked to develop maximum openness and flow, deepened by transparencies and a precision of form. In all these respects their work can also be seen as the continuing legacy of Frank Lloyd Wright and the rolling spaces of his prairie and usonian houses – his American vision of space. The maple wood and white interior also recalls something of Aalto and the Scandinavian School, and even the nature of the interiors of the American master, Richard Meier.

Hanrahan and Meyers have also written about their work and spend part of their lives in academic affiliation, teaching architecture. Their edited notes on the process of the Holley Loft are included here:

"The space of this project, which is a residence for a single person, is a loose and relatively open grid of pure formal elements which float within a non-specific and unbounded context. The loft was generated from many of the thoughts we have pursued in our practice, including notions of transparency, light, reflectivity, and freedom in the plan. These interests position our work solidly within the auspices of modern architecture, following in the traditions of Mies van der Rohe and Le Corbusier."

Holley Loft: conceptual & spatial study

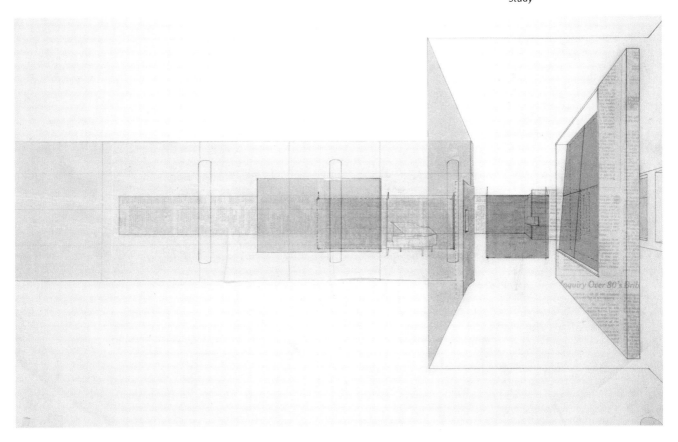

Holley Loft: main foyer & music gallery

In our pursuit of a late twentieth-century interpretation of modern architecture we have developed a sophisticated language of interpretation from which to launch our investigations. Our process of interpretation includes various visual tools, including specific types of drawings and studies which push the work in certain directions.

The frontal isometric drawing is a tool we often use. In a manner similar to perspective the frontal isometric studies interior space. Unlike perspective, however, it is mathematically precise. As Minimalists searching for conciseness in every aspect of our designs we appreciate the fact that the frontal isometric studies several things at once.

By its very nature the frontal isometric emphasizes planes. For many reasons, some of which follow, our projects deal with planes which float within and demarcate spatial terrains. The mechanics of the frontal isometric which allow us to study planar elevations simultaneously encourage the development of a planar language of space.

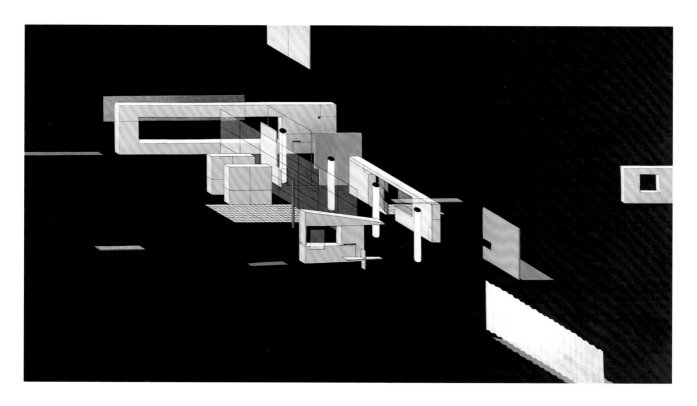

Our preoccupation with planar elements stems partly from the use of the isometric and partly from our commitment to modern space. Modern space is not specific or tightly bounded. It flows in a continuous stream and promotes a sense of connectivity between local overlapping terrains. In our architecture planes define loosely bounded areas through which the terrain of the project flows.

Walls define rooms whereas planes are discrete elements which lose their materiality and mass when seen in profile. Planes, unlike walls, loosen themselves from the edges of a specific place. Planes are not massive constructions but idealized and precisely placed constructs which, in profile, reduce to lines.

In the residential Holley Loft there was a realization of a planar language of spatial construction. There was also a realization of a programmatic intention to define a relevant language for a new architecture which is descriptive of the mediated condition of contemporary life.

Contemporary life is uniquely influenced and tempered by contemporary technologies of the modern media. These technologies allow us to be everywhere at once even as we are in one place. Expressing the unbounded spatial implications of this new condition confronts, through architecture, a significant aspect of contemporary life.

The Holley Loft is located in Manhattan and, as an expression of un-specific and unbounded space in reference to the contemporary mediated realm, there was an attempt to create readings of the Manhattan context within the loft. The space within the residence, for example, was considered as a continuation of the space of the city, uninterrupted. The final space is, however, unlike Manhattan, restful and peaceful. This residence captures the *freedom* but not the *chaos* of city life.

Holley Loft: views to living space & dining space

Holley Loft: bedroom space

Moving through the loft one feels a connection to the surrounding urban conditions. The city flows into the space through various means. The scale of the solid steel wall which masks the freight elevator, for example, is urban. The steel and glass of the skyscrapers in midtown Manhattan become walls which define sleeping areas and other scenes of domesticity such as the kitchen.

Materials are, however, strategically placed to create also moments of rest and contemplation. While the materials are urban, they also ground the interior of the loft through references to earth, gravity, and the un-manipulated materials of nature. This desire to maintain a connection to earth and gravity motivated the architects' decision to use raw, untreated steel (which is susceptible to rust), unpolished stone, and simply sealed but honestly presented maple wood.

All of these concerns are overlaid by a precise mathematical interpretation of form throughout. The plan and the elements which define the space reference the golden section, the square, and the circle. The central galleria which is also the music space is bounded by a precisely proportioned grid simultaneously based on the golden section and the twelve toned scale: a steel and glass plane which creates a visual and acoustical background for sound."

In contrast to their philosophy, attitudes, and references that relate to process, Hanrahan and Meyers' formal notes that simply describe their design and work in its material reality are equally sharp and definitive:

"The Holley Loft is an adaptation of an existing 4000 square foot industrial loft space into a residence. The space is on the second floor of a loft building in lower Manhattan."

"The design of the space evolved from a review of several of our projects that explored ambiguities between the exterior and the interior by means of partial enclosures and transparent materials, as well as discussions concerning the character and use of the space itself. As the design emerged from a series of studies over a relatively extended period of time, the character of the space began to assume a dispersed and radically open character. In the final design we were left with no solid walls. A single full-height wall of glass and steel marked the major division of master bedroom and bathroom from the rest of the apartment. At any moment, from any position, the intention is to experience the full dimension of the entire loft space, with all the elements of the domestic program distributed freely in the form of low cabinetry and movable panels. This disposition yields a complex space of constantly changing perspectives and points of view. Light from both ends of the apartment penetrates deep into the residence, while the movable panels allow for the creation of smaller, more intimate spaces to accommodate overnight guests.

The major division within the space is made by a 48 foot long raw steel and glass wall. This marks the division between the master bedroom/master bath area and the rest of the apartment with sandblasted areas for privacy. A curtain telescopes in and out from the center of the wall which is two bays of sandblasted glass. The area covered by the curtain is clear glass. The movement of the curtain allows the inhabitant of the space to control its openness.

Holley Loft: view from bedroom through library & flexible space

Opposite the steel and glass wall is a 30 foot long maple cabinet which contains an objectified fragment of the steel and glass wall plane. Here, in order to mark its displacement, the wall curves. This cabinet, which sits as an object floating in the space, also marks a boundary between the living spaces and a kitchen/guest bath. Translucent materials suspend through a wood cabinet at specific locations to partially reveal the space beyond a tautly defined planar object.

Full-height painted wood panels close down the rear of the apartment or remain in a fully open position. When they are open the panels float in the space; closed they demarcate one room; closed further, two rooms. The disposition of the space depends on the desire of the inhabitant.

The rear wall of the space is a 40 foot long bookcase and storage cabinet. This linear planar element takes on the role of a loosely defined library".

As these notes define, the central spatial device is a colonnaded Music Gallery, which – as the early collage plan shows – is intended to house a grand piano for the client, who is a pianist in leisure time. The architects have also designed furniture, such as the beautiful and simple dining table in cherry wood. The deep, earth-red rug of the living-seating area together with the natural fabrics, and currently paintings, are also part of their carefully minimal program for the ensemble.

The reality of their achievement in both space and materials is inadequately described in photographs and has to be experienced. It is breathtaking. It is also a place with a sincere warmth, and the deepest sense of sanctuary and home. On first visiting the Holley Loft, in the early evening, Louis I. Kahn's poetic reflections do adequately describe the sensation. Kahn said: 'And its feeling of being home and safe came to mind'.[9]

*Holley Loft: view from Music Gallery to dining
& living space, kitchen to left*

MoMA Tower Apartment
Thomas Hanrahan and Victoria Meyers

1998

This project is included as an exemplar of the New York Apartment, in miniature. At the same time, it also confirms the architects' commitment to an expansive spatial agenda, as the fundamental structure of the private architectural domain – a place of retreat and reflection, within, but at one remove from the relentless life of the city, without – the twenty-four hour environment of Manhattan.

The architects' own summary notes of the design, and their concept of 'swift and slow space', not only define their intentions, but in this case the means – the animations – that are integral to the realization of this work:

"This project is a renovation of a 1500 square foot apartment in the Museum of Modern Art Tower in New York. The relatively small size of the apartment required the development of an intricate set of details and innovations in space planning in order to create the sense of large and open spaces. As a complement to this idea and the small but extraordinary art collection which includes Cy Twombly, Henry Moore, and Francis Bacon, the space was composed with intense colors and materials that give a visual and tactile richness to the apartment.

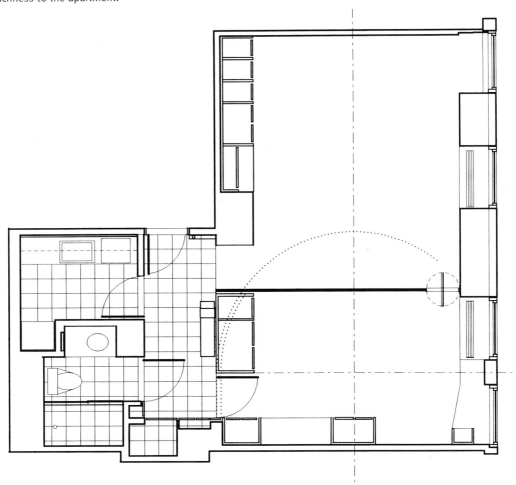

MOMA Apartment: animations

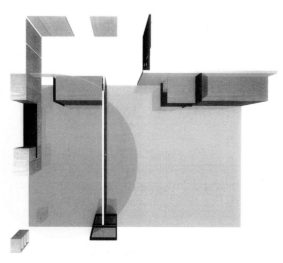

All of the walls in the apartment are finished with white plaster. The exterior envelope of the apartment is matte white plaster. The plane separating the living room and the boudoir is polished white plaster. The polished plaster wall contains a movable translucent glass plane. The combination of matte and reflective surfaces establishes within the apartment an effect of movement through a push and pull between active and inactive surfaces.

Reflective and matte surfaces establish a convocation between swift (active) and slow (inactive) space. The reflective surface of the active plane which bisects the apartment, the movable glass window inset within this plane, and the similarly framed mirror at the apartment entrance opposite establish a dialog of movement through the push and pull between these active (reflective) surfaces and the inactive (matte) surfaces of the exterior envelope.

The space was designed in the computer, through a series of rendered studies. The digital environment allowed us to view the space in movement. There is a dynamic link between the medium of these moving sketches (animations) and the spatial qualities of the final design."

As with the Holley Loft, The MoMA Apartment is essentially planar in the technique and geometry of its deep-wall installations and fit-out. The use of intense color and highly crafted furniture provides a setting for both works of art and for a placement of each element that is simple and refined.

*MOMA Apartment: entrance with
living space beyond*

The major public uses of the main space, principally those of living and dining, are thus functionally defined by the situation of the furniture, leaving the more private sleeping area as a spatial adjunct, that can be opened or closed at will, and yet united by the deep red surface of the floor plane.

Throughout the apartment, as with the Holley Loft, the detail design of each element is part of a whole limited range of materials. This includes both matte and waxed white plaster, raw and chromed steel, and white stained beech and cherrywood.

The whole arrangement of material planes and artefacts is so exact that any occupational deviation might work against the unity of the overall design. In this sense, Hanrahan and Meyers' work remains essentially Miesian in its origin. The great care the whole embodies, both for formal order and the celebration of ordinary essentials – such as a door, a seating place, an umbrella stand, or a table – is intended to elevate the experience of place, function, and spatial position.

In each instance, their architecture both receives the occupant and provides a comfortable retreat where every need is accommodated. At the same time, their pursuit of an extended spatiality is always in evidence.

MOMA Apartment: living space

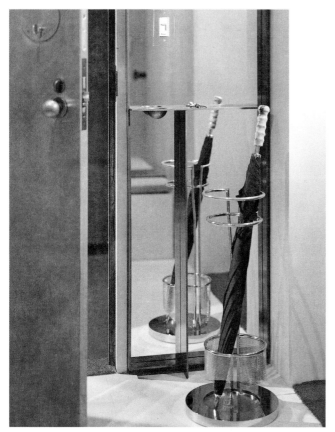

MOMA Apartment: bedroom space

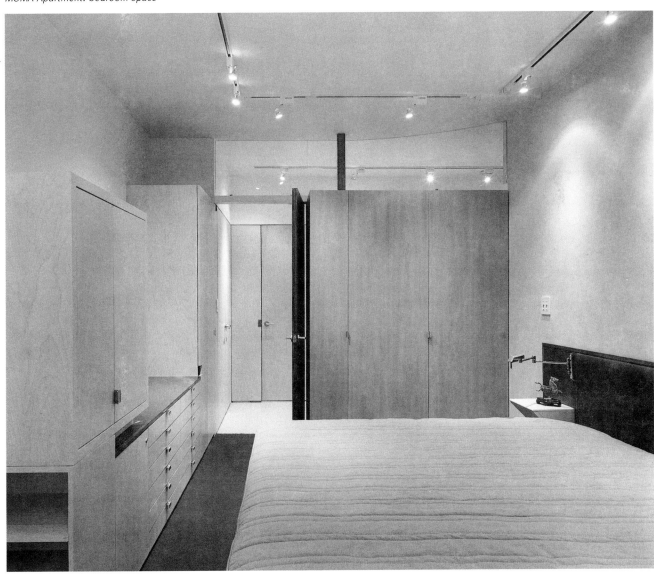

New York Apartment
Frank Lupo + Daniel Rowen

1992

The New York Apartment is a stunning, iconic project of interior architecture. At first sight, the voided white spaces, composed of a few solid and transparent planes, could be understood simply as extreme Minimalism. This is not the case. In looking at the clients' needs and intentions, it becomes clear that the project and its central focus is an abstraction – the creation of a simple condition of supreme detachment.

The space and its sparse, white material nature provide a sanctuary of reverential silence and calm. In the architects' words: 'it is a place to listen to the light, to see the silence, and to dream.'

Function and use, memory and association are removed from view in the resolution of ingenious details and fittings, and yet all human needs are beautifully served in this project – a recent masterpiece of the New York School. It is notable that there are no rooms, only spaces with numbers.

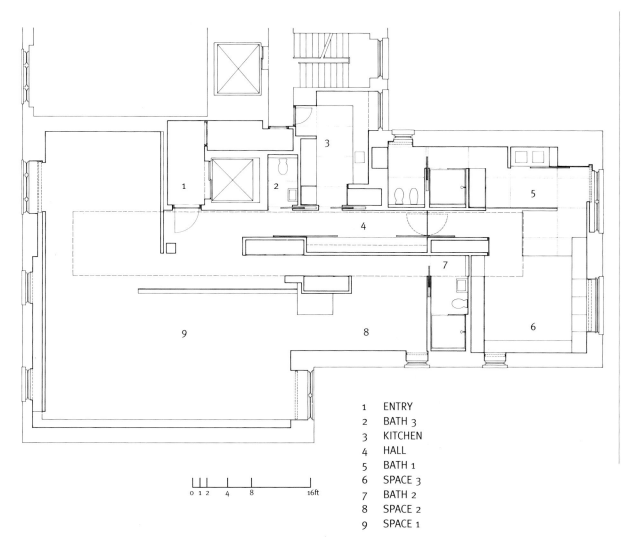

1	ENTRY
2	BATH 3
3	KITCHEN
4	HALL
5	BATH 1
6	SPACE 3
7	BATH 2
8	SPACE 2
9	SPACE 1

0 1 2   4   8   16ft

New York Apartment: principal
spaces 1 + 2 + Hall

Frank Lupo has described the apartment as 'hierarchically neutral'. He described the design process with Daniel Rowen where: 'the client pressed us to achieve a level of austerity and abstraction in their living environment' beyond anything they had previously created, for instance, in Manhattan art galleries for Larry Gagosian. Lupo summarized the principles '... to remove the contextual relationship with the city, to create a neutral environment – peaceful, sublime, Zen-like ... a Minimalist landscape ... one that eliminates even an audio sense of domesticity ... associations ... light switches ...', even the details of the shower-space eliminate all sense of conventional plumbing and drainage hardware.

Daniel Rowen's definitive notes summarize the project:

"This project transforms two traditional apartments at a white-glove Manhattan address into a 2500 square foot non-traditional pied-à-terre for a businessman and his art collection. The non-traditional aspects of the design are a result of the client's mandate that all accommodations of normal living be concealed or eliminated so that the visual field is reduced to its essence.

The abstraction of the apartment is further reinforced by the elimination of many windows, the screening of the remaining views, the absence of furniture (the soft stuff is nested behind cabinet doors), and the absence of the intended art collection. The later decision evolved as the client determined that the play of light against the compositional planes of walls, floors, and ceilings satisfied his aesthetic agenda.

The apartment's Minimalism creates a meditative landscape that radically separates it from the energies and influences of surrounding midtown Manhattan. This reductive separation affords the occupant the possibility of exploring the senses without encumbrance. In short, it is a place to listen to the light, to see the silence, and to dream."

This project is a rare combination of both an intensely motivated client and architect. The result is a triumph of restraint – a celebration of pure space.

It is perhaps noteworthy that this project, the Holley Loft and the Quandt Loft, in particular, all strive to create a form of sanctuary and retreat which is in all senses opposite to the urban forces epitomized by Manhattan itself.

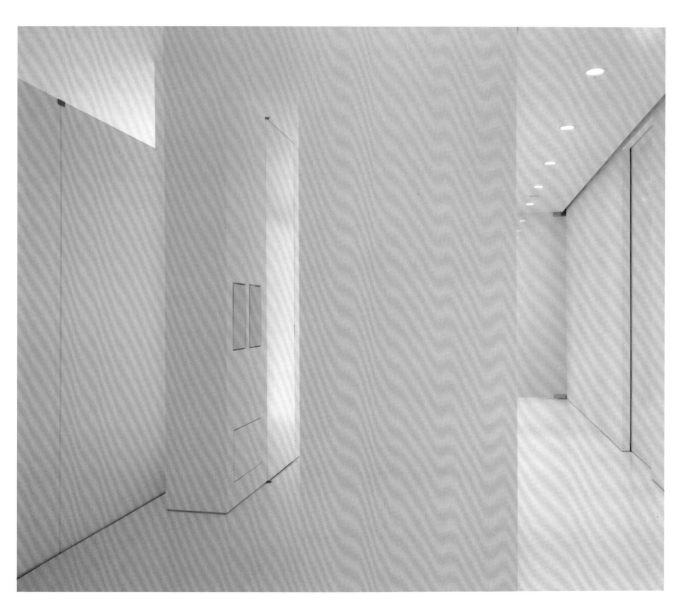

Bernard Tschumi

1987

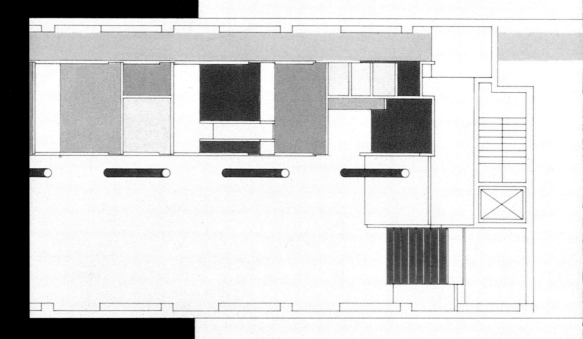

Bernard Tschumi's New York home, on West 17th Street, is a generous loft, where the proposition for his elegant transformation is centred on '...simplicity and economy ... not over-designed...'. His intention has been to maximize the potential of the space by revealing its essential length and structure, which are enhanced by the long exterior wall receiving brilliant southern daylight on its entire length, a rare condition.

Tschumi's brilliant and clear design reinforces the strength of his intellectual argument, which insists this loft project is a simple spatial condition. The fabric of the whole interior is predicated on a white shell, with ebonized oak floor throughout, coupled with polished metal and black leather furniture.

The division between public and private space is determined by sliding panels on the inner long wall. The details include the use of standard dry shop-fitting frames, with glass clerestories above the 8 foot level, adding a fusion and transparency at high level and enabling the white contained spaces to hover beneath the structural soffit.

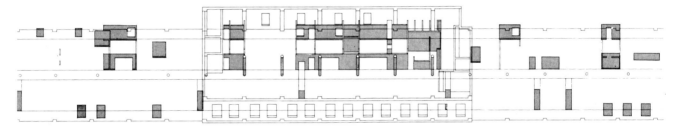

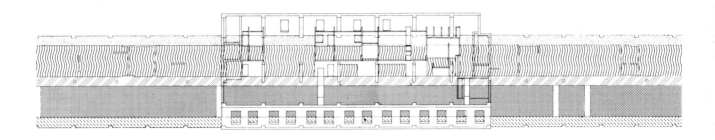

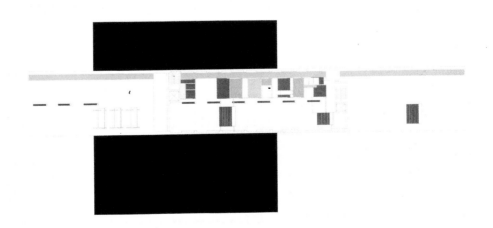

Plan transformations

17th Street Loft: view of main living space

Throughout Tschumi has used relatively cheap materials, such as standard black metal shelving elements for his vast collection of books.

Into this triumphantly simple black and white spatial enclosure, Tschumi has introduced some rare chairs by Terragni, together with a table from an industrial source and other pieces that he has retrieved and restored, originally salvage from discarded fit-outs found in various parts of New York.

The inventive intelligence and skill of this work make the so-called 'interior-decor' industry seem ridiculous. Tschumi is another architect to whom it would be superficial to apply fashionable categories, such as Minimalist. His work is a clearly principled, definitive response within the strictest and exemplary framework of modern architecture and its spatial project.

If there is, at first, a sense of déjà vu – on entering Tschumi's loft domain – it is of early, vintage Le Corbusier and more particularly Pierre Chareau and la Maison de Verre, in Paris. As Paris is also the site of Tschumi's other European studios, so the more appropriate any reference to French Modernism becomes. But, even this is unlikely and unintentional.

The Tschumi Loft is just a token gesture of one who, as a first class designer and intellect, has so focused and analyzed the project of his loft as an essential solution, that in its simplicity it is magnificent.

Tschumi's own summary exemplifies both this simplicity and the supremacy of his design:

Located in the Chelsea district of Manhattan, the 4,800 square foot loft enjoys 14 windows facing south. To keep the space as unencumbered as possible and to generate unprogrammed spaces as large as possible, all rooms needing enclosure were located in a long rectangular box inserted longitudinally in the existing envelope of the loft, thereby resulting in three parallel spatial layers, as well as in other secondary layers – all in the same direction. Full-height metal bookshelves were then located in the perpendicular direction as a mode of spatial notation. The loft was first used for work and residential purposes and is now used strictly as a private residential space.

Opposite page: 17th Street Loft: cirulation space lined with architectural projects

Rosenfeld Loft
Richard Gluckman
Gluckman Mayner Architects

1999

The Rosenfeld project represents a prime, first-rate example of both Richard Gluckman's architecture and method, and the full-scale renovation of a classic 4000 square foot Manhattan warehouse loft.

The design is dominated by a massive, linear living space of 1800 square feet, together with an integral open kitchen. The more private spaces include two bedrooms with en-suite bathroom facilities, and a study. The main bedroom has a 400 square foot outdoor roof terrace above, which also contains skylights that give natural light to the bedroom and bathroom below.

The massive shell of the warehouse forms the exterior enclosure of the loft on three principal faces and is punctured with windows, at regular intervals, providing generous daylight to all the main spaces. This existing outer wall-plane is retained and the rugged brickwork painted white, as a background for the whole design and the new insertions. The ceiling plane over much of the interior space is formed by the tilted flowing profile of the existing vaults which are plastered, and again painted white. The major floor plane throughout is a wide maple-strip installation, except in kitchen and bathrooms.

Gluckman's stringent principles of minimal intervention and sparse modernity are thus established within a supremely simple white interior volume, and unified by the natural qualities of the maple floor surface. Within this volume, a limited series of interventions is positioned, each signaled with either a rich solid, or light 'transparent' material, with white or reflective metal fittings.

The major living room spaces are defined by three principal elements. Adjacent to the kitchen, a low corner banquet of solid maple and grey upholstered cushions surrounds a 6 foot square, black walnut low table. This area is further defined by two corner wall planes of white unfinished plaster, applied over the brick shell.

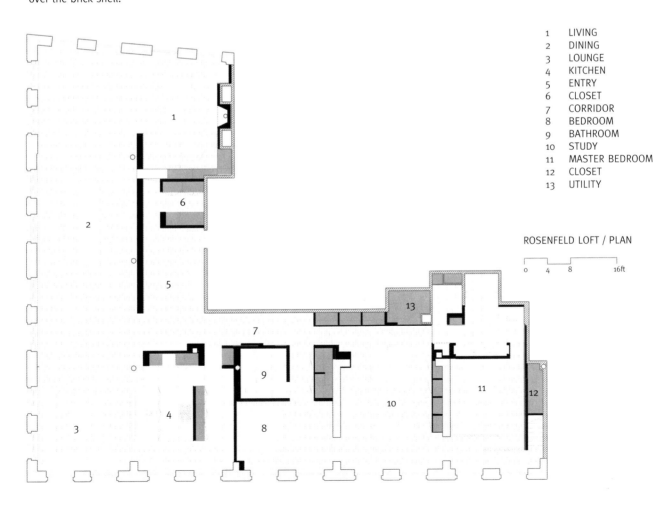

1	LIVING
2	DINING
3	LOUNGE
4	KITCHEN
5	ENTRY
6	CLOSET
7	CORRIDOR
8	BEDROOM
9	BATHROOM
10	STUDY
11	MASTER BEDROOM
12	CLOSET
13	UTILITY

ROSENFELD LOFT / PLAN

0   4   8   16ft

Grey-tinted waxed & polished plaster wall-plane defines dining space

Recessed living space & fireplace lined with red-brown makore wood panelling .

The major 'gallery' of the living space is defined by three white columns and an overhead beam, as part of the retained original structure. Recessed behind this lineage, an extended thick wall plane of grey-tinted waxed and polished plaster defines the dining area, and the entrance hall beyond. The grey reflective planar wall stands free of the vaults above and contains a battery of uplighters. This light source, and a retained silver-metal a/c duct which runs the length of the wall, both emphasize its controlling position and presence – its whole surface only penetrated once, by a salt-water aquarium, which also appears in the hall and the fireplace seating area. The dining table is a generous 15-foot-long element, in black walnut, with ten chairs. This ensemble further emphasizes the great length of the dining-galleria.

Recessed into the return corner of the plan, which is spatially indicated by the grey wall, a deep insert of cabinetry and fireplace is contained in two paneled wall-planes, forming the corner. Again these are free of the vaults and slightly lower than the grey wall, the three forming a major planar ensemble. The panelling is faced with red-brown makore wood and the fireplace mantle and plinth – two horizontals – are formed in 'absolute-black' honed marble.

Guest bedroom

At the opposite end of the major space is the free-standing kitchen and breakfast-bar with concealed pantry behind. The main elements of counter-top and screen wall are formed in white 'statuary' veined marble with a honed finish. All the fittings – such as the 'professional' gas range, cabinets, and shelves – are in contrasting polished stainless steel. Sliding doors are aluminum framed with opaque white 'lumasite' glazing. The kitchen-area floor is paved with 'fire-slate' precast concrete panels. The white marble bar is furnished with five solid maple kitchen stools. In turn, the kitchen plan-square defines the limit of the main entrance space.

Aside from the bedrooms and study space, all the main living spaces, kitchen, dining and fireplace alcove, are defined by Gluckman's technique of special installations. In turn, each of these introduces a polished exotic material – red-brown wood, grey waxed plaster, black and white marble – which, in their contrasting color and precision of surface, are deliberately juxtaposed with the basic simplicity of the white volume and maple floor plane. The use of color is restricted to white, gray and black, and the colors of natural woods.

Opposite: Dining space with kitchen & breakfast-bar far left

Gluckman's central controlling ideas of the neutral white major volume with the specific, honorific material interventions, both enhance the sweeping spatiality of the whole and at the same time, code and define the inhabitation. The sanctuary of the loft is given order and variety, and the floating nature of the inserted planes creates an inherent but restrained richness, and forms a range of internal vistas, partially dissolved in natural light, with a sense of layered transparency.

Within the private zone of the bedrooms, the study forms a central area of separation. Situated within the massive brick walls of the original structure, the fire doors – sliding metal panels – have been retained and refurbished. Otherwise the closet installations are white lacquered and the white-glazed aluminum doors are consistent throughout. The bathroom to the main bedroom is on a splendid scale, with double-shower and white marble floor; it also incorporates phenolic resin wall panels – a material Gluckman has repeatedly used. Both bedroom and bathroom are enhanced by natural top-light.

The guest bedroom is distinguished by a custom-built bed – a hovering plane of maple, with the soft upholstery overlaid on its surface.

Taken as a whole, the Rosenfeld Loft is a complete statement which contains the essence of Gluckman's architecture. While it is essentially sparse, the rich moments of his more exotic interventions not only serve as memorable highlights, but also emphasize the expansive and free nature of the interior space and light. There is an overriding and profound sense of materiality and craftsmanship, which may recall such Miesian models as the Barcelona Pavilion. But it also typifies the new tradition established by the architects of the Manhattan Loft.

Kitchen & breakfast-bar

Moss Loft

Henry Smith-Miller & Laurie Hawkinson

1990

Moss Loft

The Moss Loft is part of a series of interior architectural projects by Smith-Miller & Hawkinson, which includes the Model Apartment, the Penthouse Apartment, and the Rotunda Gallery, all of a similar date, and all involving inserts and fittings that, coupled with scaled-up rotating or sliding doors – or walls, effect both flexibility and spatial change. These concepts are all realized in a series of immaculately detailed elements, where both craft and quality of material form are effortlessly integrated with a tectonic rigor and clarity.

Their domestic work has recently been canonized in a House for a Film Producer in Los Angeles.[10] Again, while this project accepts and extends the nature of southern California on Modernism, with its spatial and constructive heritage of Mies, Neutra, and Eames, the SM+H extensions are more extreme in their planar openness and precision, extension into the landscape and endless panorama, and by what they describe as the 'transformable'. This notion runs throughout their work, and appears in microcosm in the Moss Loft.

House for a Film Producer: Los Angeles.
View of living & dining spaces

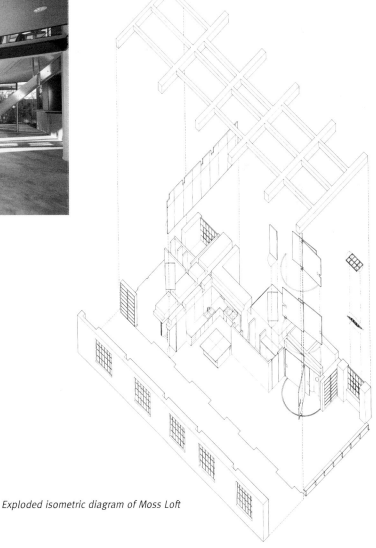

Exploded isometric diagram of Moss Loft

Henry Smith-Miller provides a personal interpretation of the Moss Loft design:

"The program for the studio and residence of a New York fashion designer, located on a nondescript floor of a midtown loft building, configures both public uses and private areas to take advantage of available light and city views.

The existing rational constructional technique of the building's structure and envelope were retained and idealized through re-proportioning and regularization to afford a more 'perfect' pre-existing condition. Factory sash steel windows were rebuilt or replaced in existing openings. A new 'level and true' white maple floor was installed over the existing wood factory sub floor. Perimeter cast iron radiation was replaced with steel pipe and fin tube radiators bracketed off the wall and in some cases integrated into steel window seats. Thus newly built could be understood as 'pre-existing'.

A series of 'new' utilitarian objects was introduced to and condition the space. A pair of very large steel doors offer introduction to the loft. Replacing the formerly static condition of the secure elevator lobby, these doors in their modulation of entry qualify and critically describe the condition of the project's program.

Moss Loft: plywood lined study & view of exterior city context.

*Moss Loft: sliding, pivot & elevator
doors at entrance*

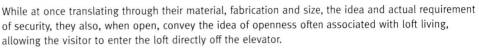

While at once translating through their material, fabrication and size, the idea and actual requirement of security, they also, when open, convey the idea of openness often associated with loft living, allowing the visitor to enter the loft directly off the elevator.

A screen wall adjacent to the dining space masks storage; a full height clear furniture grade plywood wall divides the living spaces from the bedroom and bath.

Finally, adjacent to the bedroom, with a window to the exterior, a construction grade plywood paneled study (floor, ceiling, and walls) provides an antithetical alternate to the public and re-presented 'loft', first encountered at the entry. Deliberate use of 'common' materials in the study, i.e. construction grade plywood, exposed fasteners, and the non-transparent glazing of the original window convey the constructional origins of the building's typology."

Although the Moss Loft is a relatively small project, it is a summary of the inventive and sophisticated nature of the architecture of Smith-Miller and Hawkinson, who are in the vanguard of the contemporary New York School.

Pivotal door detail

*Rotunda Gallery: Brooklyn.
Alternative conditions of main
space*

*Opposite page: Penthouse
Apartment New York 1993: View of
living & dining spaces with door /
wall & study, far right*

Tod Williams + Billie Tsien

1991

The Quandt Loft, a major 5000 square foot project in Greenwich Village, New York City, provides a residence for a jewelry designer, with her husband and two children.

It is a master-work of contemporary architecture. A mature combination of architectonic clarity, spatial freedom, and the capacity for the intimate, luxurious qualities of an elegant home combine in a design that is both simple in concept and marvellously rich and complex in detail.

The Quandt project, in itself, extends the capacity of the modern project as a whole. It also confirms the authority of its designers, the now emergent masters Tod Williams and his partner Billie Tsien, whose current work includes the sophisticated Phoenix Art Museum, in Arizona. Tod Williams, who began his career as the assistant architect to Richard Meier on the epochal Douglas House in Michigan, has brought to his own projects with Billie Tsien a controlled richness and formal harmony that are inflected by a subtle use of geometry and materials. Brought together, the architecture of the Quandt Loft is both serene and spatially dynamic.

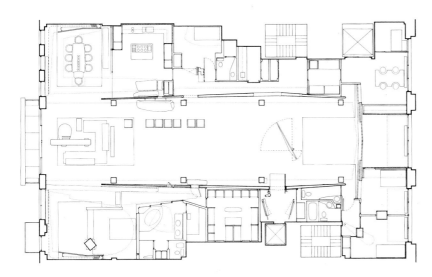

Quandt Loft: plan

Isometric view

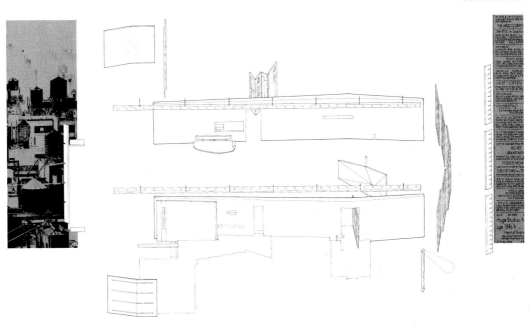

Quandt Loft: view from living space towards main bedroom area.

The design is essentially simple. A massive loft-space retains its sense of openness with a 'T'-shaped range of main living, dining, and master bedroom areas, contained between two major scalloped wall forms of self-color plaster, free of the central structural colonnade and combined with a range of sliding walls and rotating panels. The release of space in this composition is tremendous and yet its experience is calm and controlled.

The design itself is a taut, perfect composition that oscillates between austerity and richness; open and closed space, vista and containment; the isometric drawing summarizes the architectural statement, otherwise enhanced by the architect's own notes:

"The primary intention of the design of this living and work space was to preserve and enhance a strong sense of the generous loft-like space. A central terrazzo-floored living area, framed by integrally colored plaster walls, is surrounded by such functions as entrance, soldering studio, bathrooms, and kitchen. A series of sliding or rotating panels permit multiple uses and interpretations of the space making this a work of architecture which is constantly transformed by the user. While the design addresses complex programmatic requirements in a city which often feels like a battlefield, the orchestration and detailing of the architecture are such that the project is always experienced as a place of openness, serenity and freedom".

These descriptive, brief words are equally matched by the architect's own listing of the major materials and furnishings:

"Major Materials: 3-coat integrally colored plaster; skim-coated gwb; clear-anodized, and painted aluminum; satin finish stainless steel; pear wood, ebonized birch, and painted birch millwork; masonite and barra board laminated millwork, cherry wood dining chairs; leather upholstery; stained oak strip flooring; terrazzo; carved alberene stone; azul macaubus granite; emerald pearl granite; integrally colored fiberglass reinforced resin; cobalt blue laminated glass; opalescent laminated glass; translucent glass tiles; homasote; plastic laminate; silk draperies
   Furnishings: custom by architect; Ligne Rosset sofa; commissioned paintings by Gary Stephan".

The economy of means these two brief texts exhibit is countered by the complex detail development and lush blending of drapes, fixtures, and fittings integrated into the interior architecture, that is both coded and color related through the controlling wall planes, from mauve to beige self-color plaster.

Entrance & rotary screen faced in copper leaf

The sense of mobile flexibility in the design is announced at the entrance, which gives the first sight of a rotating wing-form – a copper-leaf faced folded, cantilevered plane suspended from a mast – allowing either the spatial extension or closure of the main living-gallery with its pristine terrazzo floor plane. The streamline linear steel trays suspended below ceiling level, which handle lighting fixtures, add to the thrust of the central space, as does the inward inflection of the floating wall planes. But, spatial stability is maintained by the massive structural box-columns and ebonized birch bookcases, that both bring a monumental modulation and sobriety to this magnificent loft space, terminated at the living edge by superb custom furniture and an exterior balcony.

The ever-changing patterns of daylight, mingled with the slightly colored wall planes, floor and other artefacts, together with spatial flexibility provided by sliding planes, offers the opportunity to create many scenarios, in Tod Williams' words '... many transformations are possible'.[11]

Dining space

*Bedroom space adjacent to central
reception area*

The project is deep in imagination and every detail rewards contemplation. For instance, when washing in the shower it is possible to gaze on the distant vista of the World Trade Center towers, visible through an arrow-slot that looks out over the master bedroom and its window wall. An extraordinary and poignant relationship between the extreme private realm and the landmark skyscrapers of Manhattan.

Kitchen & breakfast space

Schneider Penthouse
Gisue + Mojgan Hariri

1987

The Persian origins of the Hariri sisters are very evident in their work, above all in their sense of building as craft, and the incorporation of hand-crafted materials. This is united by a strong geometric presence and, in this case very appropriately, there is a sensuous femininity in the subtle coloration of the spaces and in the beautiful, embracing curvilinear form of their hybrid-stair masterpiece in shining steel. Their own notes concisely summarize their project and its intentions:

"This project is a renovation of a duplex loft in Soho, the art gallery center of Manhattan. It is a typical 'Artist loft' with high ceilings, particular of the cast iron, industrial buildings of this district from the turn of the century.

The intention here was to keep the characteristics of the existing loft while transforming it to develop a habitable space for the client. We kept the lower level basically open and organized the required spaces around two parallel walls. The fireplace wall and the dividing wall between the study and living area. The fireplace wall is treated with hand trawled stucco, rough in texture with a punched in log-box and a linear marble mantle.

The dividing wall is a freestanding plaster wall, which we emphasized by designing two oversized doors of steel and glass for the full size openings on either side. These doors were designed to continue the lines of the library shelving in closed position and as lighting units for the dining area in the open position.

Upper plan

Floor plan

Resolving the vertical circulation between the two levels created a challenging situation in replacing the existing spiral stair. Due to the number of rotations and open grating treads, the existing spiral vibrated beyond the norm and caused a frightening experience going up and down. However we were not allowed to enlarge the opening (5ftx5ft) in the ceiling to accommodate for a larger stair. After many attempts, we came up with a hybrid stair, partially straight and partially spiral.

The two stairs are structurally independent but are unified with a single sheet of steel curving in a logarithmic spiral. The experience of moving through this stair is like being on a Mobias Strip. One is simultaneously inside and outside of the steel sheet. The stair railings terminate in a circular pattern of rings which gets carried into the design of the pendant light fixture and bar stools.

Opposite page: Schneider Penthouse:
bar & spiral hybrid staircase

The bar unit shields the kitchen, using similar materials, while introducing color via its blue azul macaubus marble counter and mahogany support. The owner's passion for the color blue is accommodated throughout the loft in a variety of shades. The wood floors are stained in light blue-gray while the library walls are in deep Florentine blue and the doors are painted steel-blue.

Main living space

Roof terrace at bedroom level

On the upper level, where the master suite and the roof-garden are located, the blue tint is softer. The roof-garden is composed with a rose arbor and a wisteria trellis, all made of cedar wood and a spiral stair completing one's journey upward terminating in the private sun deck area above.

Reflecting on their earlier life in Iran itself, Gisue Hariri has emphasized that '... art and science are intertwined, especially in buildings. Design and poetry are very important parts of everyday life ...' and in relation to the Hariri sisters' work as a whole '... ultimately, the goal in our work is peace, quietness, harmony'.

After some ten years of daily life in her SoHo penthouse, Kathleen Schneider, founder of her nearby Children's Museum of Arts, confirmed her own appreciation of the great qualities of her home, which is a testament to the gifts of spatiality and crafted materiality the Hariri's dedicate in their architecture.

Master Suite detail

Gisue and Mojgan Hariri's lecture on Philosophy of Architecture, given at The Architectural League in 1990,[12] states their position:

"We do not believe in Chaos, we do not follow Trends, and we despise Kitsch.

It is the intention of our work to bring together in an equilibrium the Mind that disintegrates and categorizes and the Soul that is in constant search for universal unity of all things and events.
We believe that all opposites are polar, but at the same time only different aspects of the same phenomenon; that all opposites are interdependent and their conflict can never result in a total victory of one side and the result can only be a manifestation of the interplay between the two.
Examples of this concept 'The Unification of the Opposites' can be found in modern physics at the sub-atomic level where particles are both destructible and indestructible; where matter is both continuous and discontinuous, and force and matter are different aspects of the same phenomenon. Life in general and Architecture in particular are like force and matter intertwined. It is the events and the smallest experiences in life that form Visions of architecture".

Ten years or so after the Schneider project, to define the Hariris as New Minimalists, therefore, would be totally superficial and inappropriate. Their thought and their work run much deeper than that.
While their architecture, and its material and spatial content, subscribes to the central traditions of the modern project, in its response there is another resonance. Carried forward from the spiritual simplicity of their ancient culture and its beautiful forms, order and material strength, the Hariris have established their own version of an historically inflected, utterly personal and inhabitable modern architecture. An architecture of essential simplicity. But it is also incised with the modern craft of Carlo Scarpa and the contemporary parallel in New York, in the works of Steven Holl.

'Zeroness … [is] a spiritual quality. We know when it's there, but we don't know how we get it'[13]
Gisue and Mojgan Hariri, New York, February 1997.

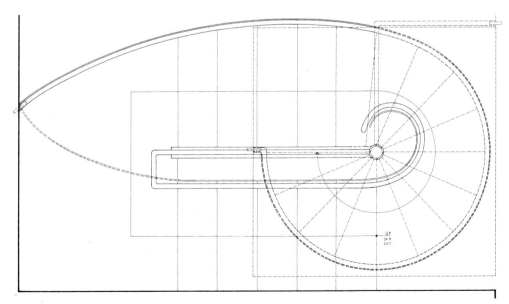

Hybrid stair: plan

Chelsea Loft

Scott Marble + Karen Fairbanks

1996

The Chelsea Loft contains both the ideas of flexibility and the concentration of the major spaces that receive natural light. The second principle is extended into the details of the overall installation.

The architects' notes further emphasize these principles and the organization of the spaces:

"This project is a residential loft designed for a family of four with a typically urban lifestyle. This was the third project we had completed for them and we were exploring variations on recurring themes from our previous designs – the flexibility of the home to adjust to changing lifestyles, the articulation of specific domestic activities within a highly flexible organization, and the innovative use of unexpected materials. These interests were shared by the clients and served as a point of departure for the design.

Domestic space has persistently expanded into abandoned and obsolete buildings as industry and manufacturing, and more recently financial and corporate businesses, have moved out of the city. Industrial lofts inhabited as domestic space are a uniquely urban condition which in New York have become common and highly desirable due to their generous size and openness. This loft is located in an early twentieth-century industrial building in Chelsea that, like many buildings of this type in New York, has evolved into a residential cooperative. The neighborhood is a mix of residential and commercial uses, with a new influx of art galleries relocating from Soho. Given the typical lot within the Manhattan grid, this building is unusual due to its longitudinal orientation parallel to the street and exceptional for its southern exposure with numerous large windows.

The organization is generated from an interest in the possibility of multiple spatial and programmatic relationships that can be configured according to the type and scale of the activity. Although areas are designated for specific domestic functions (such as living, dining, breakfast area, family living, study,

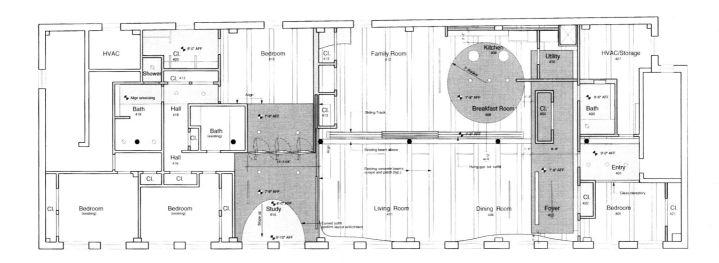

and sleeping), a series of four large sliding screens and three pivoting doors transforms individual areas into continuous space allowing activities to freely interact. The loft is generally organized around a flexible relationship between formal and informal living spaces defined by the positions of the screens. Floor patterns and materials and ceiling elements run between adjacent rooms reinforcing specific connections between related activities. A cork floor and low ceilings in the study continue into the parents' bedroom, making a link that is regulated by the pivot doors. The kitchen and breakfast rooms are linked by a low circular soffit overhead.

Flexible relationship between spaces

Closed sleeping space

Kitchen, family space & dining area connected beyond, with screens open

Living & dining area with screens closed

The orientation of the building parallel to the street and the resulting long shadows cast by the window bays inspired the specific design of the moving panels. The diagonal lines formed by the overlap of fibreboard and glass are both an abstraction and continuation of the shadows cast through the space. At certain times of the day, shadows cross the floor and bend up the face of the panels combining with the diagonal lines to form a collage of light and pattern and a perspective illusion of a continuous space.

View into kitchen & family space with screens open

The project is based on an economy which uses few elements to establish multiple conditions. We were interested in a Minimalism through the abstract use of materials, allowing them to be understood as surfaces without emphasizing their joints and connections. We collaborated closely with the fabricator of the sliding screens and pivoting doors detailing them to support those ideas. The sliding screens are medium density fibreboard (MDF) and translucent glass. Each screen is uniquely configured, making their visual composition and physical weight distribution different. The glass in the screen slips between the MDF panels becoming the structural connection from one section of fibreboard to another. The pivoting doors are MDF, translucent glass, and aluminum forming a three dimensional parallelogram. The aluminum panels have two circular cutouts allowing light to pass through the doors while simultaneously providing structure for the asymmetrical pivot. Other materials used include maple, walnut, cork, and linoleum floors, dyed ash kitchen cabinets, a black granite countertop, and a translucent glass backsplash".

The extended length of dining & living space which receives generous natural light

O/K Apartment
Sulan Kolatan + William MacDonald

1997

The work of Kolatan and MacDonald is hallmarked by their intention to extend the experiential nature of their designs, often within a limited framework. The O/K Apartment summarizes their interior explorations and their own extension of their design principles:

"This project involved the remodelling and combining of two separate but contiguous apartments totalling 1,500 square feet. The West Side Building was originally built as artists' ateliers and residences. The owners asked for flexibility in the use of the apartment's configurations so that it could be used both as a corporate apartment, and serve as a private pied-à-terre. Three sleeping areas with variable degrees of privacy respond to this need. A series of panels serve either to divide the space in half, or unfolds into a grand dinner table for entertaining.

The 'domestic spaces' are modar structures with integral color dye fabricated from information in digital format. Other materials include epoxy, aluminum laminated plywood, concrete, cementitious board, stainless steel. The project was built in 1996-97.

The interior project was conceived somewhat in the manner of a 'miniature urbanism' consisting of three phases: **1** – identification of individual 'sites' within the existing space (locations for new structures referred to as 'domestic scapes'), **2** – generation of these structures through cross-profiling, and **3** – mapping of similarities akin to co-citation mapping.

Computer rendered plan

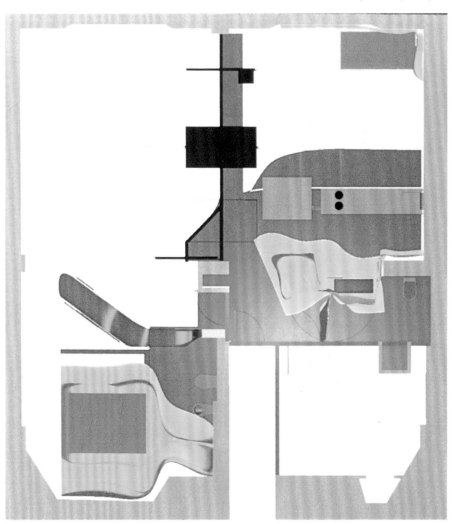

Flexibility of configuration

For the generation of the new structures on each site, section profiles of everyday domestic objects and furnishings were electronically cross-referenced with each other regardless of original scale and category but with an interest in registering formal and operational similarities between them. Based on this information, they were then spatially organized and resurfaced. The resulting structures are chimerical in the sense that the initial profiles as indexes of particular identities (bed, sink, sofas, etc.) are now inextricably embedded within an entirely new entity which they have helped produce. We will loosely refer to this new entity as a 'domestic scape', or synthetic topography.

The 'domestic scape', unlike the domestic space (the room) or the domestic object (the piece of furniture), cannot be sufficiently identified by categoric classification. Rather, like a particular landscape, its identification is contingent on the presence of a set of idiosyncratic features. As the discussion of identity is linked here to the question of programmatic performance, it is useful to continue the landscape analogy in evaluating the synthetic topography. In the instance of the bed, this would mean that a 'plateau' measuring a minimum of a x b square feet can be identified as but would not be limited to a potential sleeping area. This is very different from the concept of a 'bedroom' or a 'bed' which are both categoric designations of identity, and therefore fixed in their programmatic associations.

Panels unfolded to form a large dinner table

The formal and programmatic conditions thus obtained are unknown and impossible to preconceive or predict. The excess of (in)formation poses an interesting problem in as much as it is ambiguous and therefore open to interpretation on many levels. The resulting synthetic topographies, unlike conventional subdivisions by rooms, do not register legible distinctions between spaces or between programs. The 'domestic scapes' are always situated across the boundaries of the existing domestic spaces. The bed/bath scape, for example, forms a continuous surface within its own limits. One of the excesses produced here is the seamless transformation between the space shaped by the 'bathtub' and the bedroom floor/wall. A door into the 'bathtub' is sealed as the water level rises, pressing against it.

While the topographic model is useful in understanding certain aspects of these structures, it is important to note that the surface in this case is not just terrain, a top layer with a fairly shallow sectional relief, but deep – both in a conceptual and literal sense. Conceptually, this term is used to denote the possibility of an increased range. The surface is not exclusively thought as thin, shallow, external, etc. but as capable of incorporating degrees of cavitation, inclusion, thickening, 3D spatial enveloping, interiority, and so on. Considered in this way, the relation between deep and shallow, space and surface, is not as defined as a dichotomy, but within the terms of transformation. It is this capacity of the scape to change incrementally and continuously that produces a chimerical condition between furniture, space, and surface. Conventional assumptions about the codification of the interior surfaces as floors, walls, and ceilings do not always hold here. At the least, the place and manner in which these constituent elements meet is redefined.

In the final phase of the project these individual scapes are interconnected across the space of the apartment in a manner similar to co-citation mapping (electronic literary indexing). This kind of similarity mapping yields both an analysis of already existing relations by indicating the co-presence of certain idiosyncrasies across or regardless of type as well as relational method of production. One which produces simultaneous effects across an established network. An electronic web of second-iteration-sites is constructed with the intent to map similarities and differences between heretofore unrelated entities. The individual sites are bound together as a system in which small scale manipulations affect changes throughout at varying scales and locales".

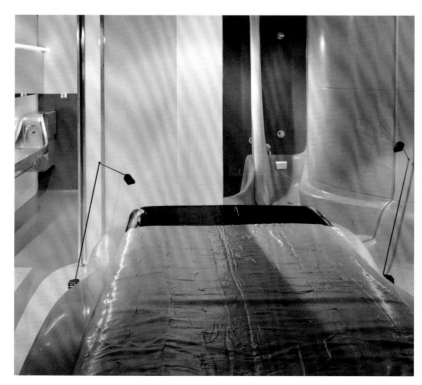

Bed / bath scape details

'K' Loft
George Ranalli

1995

The 'K' Loft by George Ranalli is a personal translation of the Manhattan loft that carries with it a sense of the 'homecoming' that is embodied in the work of Frank Lloyd Wright. His sense of both materials and space is summarized in this project, and the following notes are a concise gathering of the major ideas:

"This project is for the renovation of a 2100 square foot loft in the Chelsea section of New York City for two artists and their son. The existing space is a brick room with exposed brick bearing walls running the length of the space and a brick ceiling. The ceiling is a series of brick vaults spanning steel sections from the front to the back of the loft. The existing room is a compelling space.
  A series of new forms is designed for the loft which accommodates the owner's program. These new shapes contain two new bedrooms, a new master bedroom, a new kitchen, and a second bathroom. It was also the owner's intention that the feeling and the quality of the original loft be maintained while designing the new spaces.

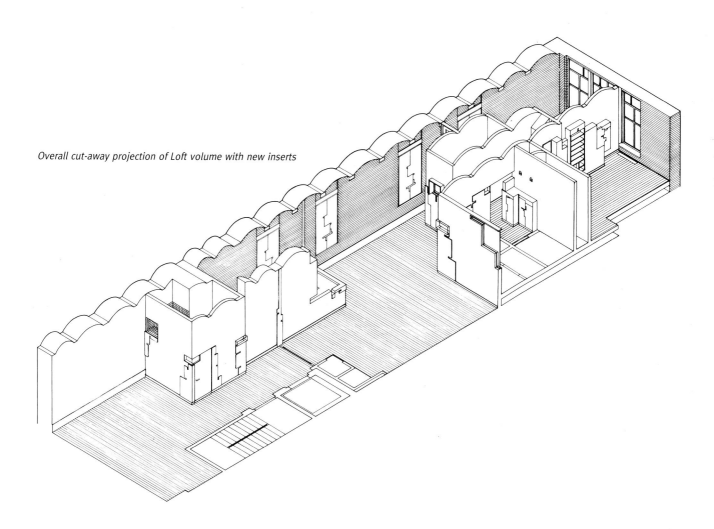

Overall cut-away projection of Loft volume with new inserts

Major end-space defined by insertion of new volumetric container

*View through cental living space of
Loft volume with retained brick vaults
– bedroom containers beyond*

A secondary scale of detail:
corners protected with irregular –
profile birch plywood panels &
fixed with a pattern of screw-
fasteners

The solution as built features a series of volumes sitting in the loft which allow the space of the room to remain continuous. Each of the volumes takes a key position in the space so that it contains space as well as producing space between the forms. The elements are made in plaster which then have some fixed translucent glass inserted in the blocks. The corners are protected with large panels of birch plywood which are cut in irregular profiles to help establish a second range of scale to the rooms. These panels are affixed to the plaster walls with a pattern of screw fasteners. All doors, lamps, cabinets, and other decorative objects are custom designed as part of the project.

The owner's other criteria was to complete the project for a budget that was acceptable to them. The project was completed within the owner's desired amount."

Kitchen aside to main living / dining area

Raised stepped access to bedrooms

Urban context of Loft

Volumetric inserts exploit detail &
light within the original brick shell

1

Slesin Suzanne, Cliff Stafford & Rozensztroch Daniel 'The International Book of Lofts', Clarkson N. Potter Inc. New York 1986, contains an international survey of lofts and their interiors, together with a general introductory history from early loft dwellers, through the expansion of loft dwelling in the 1970s to the mid '80s. The survey includes a huge variety of interior designs and furnishing.

2

Sorkin Michael, Holl Steven (essays) in 'Alan Buchsbaum 1935-1987', The Monacelli Press Inc. New York 1996, exemplifies the comprehensive monograph on the work of a single designer whose brilliant career included a range of famous clients such as Rosalind Krauss, Billy Joel, Bett Midler and many others. Buchsbaum's work included a series of inventive loft interiors with furniture and carpets custom designed. His own flamboyant Lofts 1 of 1976, and Loft 2 included his hallmark use of airport run-way lighting.

3

The author is indebted to Victoria Meyers, of Hanrahan and Meyers, for consistent and valuable advice, and for many introductions to architects whose work had not formerly come to our attention. If there is a coherence in the corpus of work presented, it lies in a common background, whose rigour and simplicity of purpose are rooted in the intellectual traditions of the Cambridge School, England, U.K., which we both share.

4

Merkel Jayne, 'The new minimalism', Oculus, AIA New York Chapter Vol. 59, no. 5, January 1997, p.9, refers to this development of modernism: "...the interest in the spare geometry of minimalism suggests an interest in subtlety, the basic components of design, and an awakening of an architectural sensibility, as opposed to the decorator's undisciplined largesse."

5

The architects, in conversation with the author, explained their brief which centred on a theory of neutral hierarchy; the creation of a suspended spatial condition that removed associations with both objects and exterior city context, thus forming the basis for a pure sense of sanctum, refuge and spiritual renewal.

6

George Ranalli was responsible for the reconstruction in drawings and models of Frank Lloyd Wright's projects featured in the 1996 exhibition at the Canadian Center for Architecture, CCA Montreal, Canada. See catalogue: íFrank Lloyd Wright: Designs for an American Landscape 1922-1932í, CCA Montreal, 1996.

7

George Ranalli produced models and an installation for the recent Carlo Scarpa exhibition at the Canadian Center for Architecture, and contributed an essay to the catalogue, 'Carlo Scarpa: Intervening with History', CCA Montreal, 1999.

8

See Ranalli, George, Buildings and Projects, Princeton Architectural Press, 1988, for a full review of Ranalli's architectural production of drawings.

9

Johnson, Nell E. 'Light is the Theme: Louis I. Kahn and the Kimbell Art Musuem' Comments on Architecture by Louis Kahn Kimbell Art Foundation, Forth Worth, Texas 1975, p.33.

10

Frampton, Kenneth, and Larkin, David, 'The Twentieth Century American House: Masterworks of Residential Architecture', 1995 Rizzoli and Thames & Hudson, pp.253-261 includes a full illustrated review of SM&H's extensions to an earlier 'Case Study' house of the 60s era.

11

Pearson, Clifford A., 'Balancing Act' Architectural Record Interiors 9/1991 p.111, records a discussion with Tod Williams.

12

Lecture by the Hariris at the Architectural League, New York, 26 April 1990, as part of their competition success, the Young Architects Forum 1990, sponsored by the League.
By this time, 1990, "...the sisters had earned a cult following." Fisher, Laura, 'House of Hariri' AVENUE, June/July 1996.

13

Jacobs, Karrie, Cityscape, 'Sub-Minimal Message' New York Magazine, 24 February 1997, p.38, contains the interview with Gisue & Mojgan Hariri where this quotation is placed.

Biographies

Hanrahan & Meyers

Lupo & Rowen

Bernard Tschumi

Richard Gluckman

Smith-Miller & Hawkinson

Williams & Tsien

Hariri & Hariri

Marble & Fairbanks

Kolatan & MacDonald

George Ranalli

Hanrahan & Meyers, Architects

Thomas Hanrahan and Victoria Meyers have practiced in Manhattan since 1985. Their work includes projects of many scales and diverse programs. In all of their projects they seek a balance between the precision of architectural form and the dynamic and contingent forces that create unexpected spaces and experiences. While their work shows great attention to detail and clear architectonic expression, elements of chance, action, and urban context are introduced into the design process as a means of bringing contemporary culture into their designs. Within this framework their built projects range from residences to public buildings. In 1993 they received the commission for the AIA New York Chapter Headquarters after submitting a winning design in a limited competition. In 1995 their design for a new residential loft in Manhattan received wide-ranging press attention, including *Harper's Bazaar* and *Architectural Record*. Their current projects include two community centers for the New York City Housing Authority, and a master plan study for the Battery Park City Authority.

Victoria Meyers was born in Abilene, Texas in 1952. She attended Lafayette College in Pennsylvania where she received a B.A. in Art History / Civil Engineering in 1978. In 1982 she received a M.Arch, from Harvard's Graduate School of Design. Her work in architecture reflects a broadly based cross-disciplinary background. In her work Victoria references influences outside the discipline of architecture reaching into the other arts and mathematical theory to broaden the base of her design aesthetic. Her apprenticeship in the office of the British architect, Richard Rogers, exposed her to the use and detailing of steel, glass, and concrete. She continues to pursue these and other modern method materials in her work. In addition to her practice Victoria also teaches architecture at Columbia's Graduate School of Architecture, Planning and Preservation.

Thomas Hanrahan was born in Chicago, Illinois in 1956. He attended the University of Illinois at Urbana-Champaign where he received his B.S.Arch, in 1978. In 1983 he received his M.Arch, from Harvard's Graduate School of Design. In 1978 he studied in Versailles, France and in 1984 he traveled through central and northern Europe investigating modern European design under a Wheelwright Fellowship from Harvard University. These experiences have been decisive in formulating his interest in an experimental design method reflecting modern life and culture and his interest in the crafting of materials. Thomas also brings experience in the planning of large-scale projects, first with Skidmore, Owings, and Merrill, Architects, in Chicago, and most recently in private practice in New York as Hanrahan and Meyers' projects have increased in scope and complexity. Thomas Hanrahan has taught at Columbia University, Harvard University, and Yale University. He is currently Dean of the Pratt Institute School of Architecture.

Frank Lupo & Daniel Rowen
Frank Lupo

Frank Lupo has recently joined the firm of Perkins & Will, New York, as Associate Principal, in the position of Director of Design. A graduate of the University of Cincinnati with a Master of Architecture from Yale University, he began his career with Studio Works, Morphosis and Gwathmey Siegel & Associates, before becoming a partner with Lupo Rowen Architects. Immediately prior to joining Perkins & Will, he was an Associate at Skidmore Owings and Merrill in New York. He is currently President of The Architectural League of New York, and has also served as a faculty member and design critic for Cooper Union and Harvard Graduate School of Architects, and is a juror for Columbia University.

Daniel Rowen

Daniel Rowen is currently the principal of Daniel Rowen Architect Plc, an architectural practice located in New York City and established in 1994. A graduate from Brown University with a Masters of Architecture degree from Yale University, he began his career with Gwathmey Siegel & Associates, and was a partner with Lupo Rowen Architects from 1985 to 1994. He has also served as a faculty member at the Graduate School of Architecture & Planning at Columbia University and has been a design critic at the Harvard, Yale, and University of Pennsylvania schools of architecture.

The work of the office and of Lupo Rowen Architects has received numerous local and national design awards and has been published internationally. Projects have been exhibited in the Deutsches Architekturmuseum, the National Academy of Design, and the Museum of Modern Art.

Bernard Tschumi

A permanent US resident who holds both French and Swiss nationalities, Bernard Tschumi came to the United States from London in 1976. His work was exhibited at the time in a number of galleries, including Artists Space and PS1 in New York; indeed, Tschumi's 1976 show, 'Architectural Manifestos', at Artists Space may be the first exhibition of work by an architect in an art gallery or alternative space. In 1983, he won the prestigious competition to design the Parc de la Villette, a 125-acre, $300 million public park containing dramatic buildings, walkways, bridges, and numerous gardens at the northeast edge of Paris. Today, over 8 million people visit La Villette every year, exceeding the attendance figures of EuroDisney. Tschumi established his Paris office in 1983 with the commission for La Villette, followed by the New York office in 1988. Today, projects that are completed or under construction include Le Fresnoy National Studio for Contemporary Arts, in Tourcoing, France, a major facility housing film and video production studios, cinemas, performance and exhibition space, restaurants, housing for post-graduate students and faculty, and administrative offices (opened 1997); Columbia University's new 225,000-square-foot Lerner Hall Student Center, built in association with Gruzen Samton Architects, which contains a 1500-seat auditorium and a 400-seat cinema, lounges, dining and club rooms, a bookstore, classrooms, and offices (opening in fall 1999); the 275,000-square-foot Marne La Vallee School of Architecture for 1200 students in Champs-sur-Marne, a suburb of Paris (to open in fall 1999); the Interface Flon, a bus, train, and subway station and a pedestrian bridge in Lausanne, Switzerland, (to open in the year 2000); and a 7,000-seat/70,000-square-foot Concert Hall and Exhibition Complex in Rouen, situated 70 miles northwest of Paris (to be completed by fall 2000). Most recently, Tschumi won First Prize in the competition to build the new 100,000-square-foot Florida International University School of Architecture in Miami, FL with local architects, Bruno-Elias & Associates. In addition, he was one of the three finalists selected by The Museum of Modern Art in New York in 1997 to design its new expansion.

Tschumi studied in Paris and at the Federal Institute of Technology (ETH) in Zurich, Switzerland, from which he received his degree in 1963. He taught at the Architectural Association in London (1970-79), the Institute for Architecture and Urban Studies in New York (1976), Princeton University (1976 and 1980) and the Cooper Union (1981-3). Since 1988 he has been Dean of the Graduate School of Architecture, Planning and Preservation at Columbia University in New York.

Tschumi is a member of the College International de Philosophie in France and the recipient of many distinguished honors, including the Legion d'Honneur, bestowed on him in a special ceremony by President François Mitterand, and the Ordre des Arts et Lettres. He was awarded France's Grand Prix National d'Architecture in 1996 and has received England's Royal Victoria Medal, as well as awards from the American Institute of Architects and the National Endowment for the Arts. His architectural work has been widely exhibited throughout Europe and the United States. He is the author of numerous articles and several books, including *Event-Cities* (1994) and *Architecture and Disjunction* (1994), in their fifth and fourth printing respectively; and *The Manhattan Transcripts* (1981, re-issued 1994). A book chronicling the design and construction of Le Fresnoy, titled *Tschumi: Le Fresnoy Architecture In/Between* has been published in 1999 by The Monacelli Press.

Tschumi is a member of the American Institute of Architects and the Ordre des Architects in France, and is licensed to practice in the State of New York and throughout Europe. He is the head of the firm Bernard Tschumi Architects, with offices in New York and Paris.

Richard Gluckman & David Mayner

The firm of Gluckman Mayner Architects is the successor firm to Richard Gluckman Architects, formed in New York in 1977. The firm has undertaken a wide range of residential, commercial, and institutional projects throughout the United States, Great Britain, Spain, and the People's Republic of China.

The firm has worked for the Dia Center for the Arts for the past 19 years, converting numerous industrial buildings into exhibition, storage, and administrative spaces. These projects have ranged from the design of single spaces for permanent installations to the design for Dia's main exhibition space at 548 West 22nd Street, which was opened in 1987 and received an award from the American Institute of Architects.

Gluckman Mayner's commissions have included: The Andy Warhol Museum in Pittsburgh (1994); Site Santa Fe, an exhibition facility in New Mexico (1995)' renovation of the Carnegie Institute's European and American art galleries as well as exhibition design for the 'Carnegie International' in Pittsburgh (1995); renovation of the contemporary galleries for the Museum of Fine Arts, Boston (1989); the 1995 'Brancusi' and 1996 'Cezanne' retrospectives at the Philadelphia Museum of Art; and the expansion and renovation of exhibition space and administrative offices for the Whitney Museum (1997). Gluckman has designed numerous commercial galleries in the United States, most recently Mary

Boone Gallery, on Fifth Avenue, and the Paula Cooper Gallery, on West 21st Street. Work has also been completed on a renovation to an existing building and an addition of a two-storey building for The Georgia O'Keeffe Museum in Santa Fe. Recently the firm was selected for two major new projects: the new Austin Museum of Art, a $35 million project that is meant to become a focal point in Austin's cultural life; and The North Carolina Museum of Art's 40 million dollar expansion and renovation. Richard Gluckman received a Bachelor of Arts degree from Syracuse University in 1970, and a Master of Architecture from Syracuse in 1971. He was a visiting critic at Harvard University's Graduate School of Design in 1989 and 1995. In 1998 he became a fellow of the American Institute of Architects.

In January 1998, David Mayner was named a partner in the newly constituted firm of Gluckman Mayner Architects. This partnership is the culmination of David Mayner's 18 years of association with Richard Gluckman and followed the completion of the widely acclaimed Whitney Museum of American Art expansion project in New York City, which he oversaw. Before joining Richard Gluckman Architects in 1980, David was employed by the firm of Skidmore, Owings, Merrill, New York. Prior to that he worked for the office of Denninger and Jann Bonn, Germany, and Lumatec in Munich, a manufacturer of lighting technology.

Smith-Miller & Hawkinson
Laurie Hawkinson

An architect and principal in the office of Smith-Miller & Hawkinson; she received her Masters in Fine Arts from the University of California at Berkeley, then attended the Whitney Independent Study Program in New York and received her Professional Degree in Architecture from The Cooper Union in 1983. Currently an Assistant Professor of Architecture at Columbia University, Laurie Hawkinson has held visiting adjunct professor positions at SCI-Arc, Harvard University, Yale University, Parsons School of Design, and the University of Miami. She is a board member of the Architectural League of New York, a member of the Board of Governors of the New York Foundation for the Arts, and has served as a panelist for the New York State Council on the Arts in Architecture, Planning and Design from 1986-9. Collaborative projects include the North Carolina Museum of Art 'Master' Site Plan and project, now built, for an outdoor cinema and ampitheater with artist Barbara Kruger and landscape architect Nicholas Quennell, LA Arts Park Competition, and the Seattle Waterfront Project, also with Kruger and Quennell. She has worked with the artist Silvia Kolbowski on a project for the Wexner Center's recent exhibition on suburbia, House Rules.

Henry Smith-Miller

An Architect and principal in the office of Smith-Miller & Hawkinson; he began his private practice in 1977 following a seven year association with Richard Meier and Associates where he was a project architect for several nationally recognized architectural projects: The Atheneum at New Harmony, Indiana, the Albany Mall Art Museum, and the Bronx Development Center. He received an undergraduate degree from Princeton University, a Masters in Architecture from the Graduate School of Architecture at the University of Pennsylvania, and a Fulbright Grant to study architecture in Rome, Italy. Henry Smith-Miller has held adjunct professor positions at Columbia University, the City University of New York, the University of Virginia, the University of Pennsylvania, Harvard University, has been Thomas Jefferson Professor in Architecture at the University of Virginia, and has held the Saarinen Chair at Yale University. He has recently taught a graduate studio with Kenneth Frampton at Columbia University. He has also served on the Board of Creative Time and is a member of the Associate Council of the Museum of Modern Art in New York. Collaborative projects include the exhibition design for Discontinuous Space: Projects by Smith-Miller & Hawkinson Architects with artist Silvia Kolbowski. He is a registered architect in New York, Pennsylvania, Maryland, Connecticut, California, North Carolina, Virginia, Maine, Colorado, holding NCARB Certification.

Tod Williams Billie Tsien and Associates

Tod Williams

Tod Williams received his BA in 1965 and MFA in 1967 from Princeton University. Although known primarily for built work, he has a longstanding commitment to teaching and theoretical issues. After six years as Associate Architect in the office of Richard Meier, he began his own practice in 1974. He taught at the Cooper Union for more than 15 years and has also taught at Harvard, Yale, the University of Virginia, Southern California Institute of Architecture, Columbia University and RISD. He has held the Thomas Jefferson Professorship at the University of Virginia. In 1995 he was appointed to the Ruth Carter Stevenson Endowed Regents Chair at the University of Texas at Austin. Recipient of a Mid-Career Prix de Rome 1983, his buildings, writings, and teachings are based on the examination of the physical and philosophical nature of construction – the 'Art of Building'. In 1992 he was honored by becoming a Fellow of the American Institute of Architects.

Billie Tsien

Billie Tsien is a graduate of Yale University in Fine Arts. She received her Masters in Architecture from UCLA in 1977. Her work has always bridged the two worlds of fine art and architecture. She has taught at Parsons School of Design, Southern California Institute of Architecture, Harvard, and Yale. In 1995 she held the O'Neil Ford Chair at the University of Texas at Austin. With Tod Williams, she has been the recipient of several grants from the New York State Council of Arts and the National Endowment of the Arts. These grants were used to fund collaborations with artists Jackie Ferrara, Mary Miss, Dan Graham, and Elyn Zimmerman. She is on the Board of the Public Arts Fund, the Architectural League and is a vice president of the Municipal Arts Society.

Widely published works of Williams and Tsien include The Spiegel Pool House, Feinberg Hall at Princeton University and the Downtown Branch of the Whitney Museum of American Art. These projects, as well as several others, have all received New York Chapter AIA Distinguished Architecture Awards. Feinberg Hall and the Spiegel Pool House were chosen to receive National AIA Honor Awards in 1988 and 1989, and the Quandt Loft and the Go Silk Showroom in New York City received National AIA Interior Honor Awards in 1992 and 1993. Williams and Tsien have been awarded the New York Chapter 1996 Medal of Honor from the AIA. They were also awarded the Arnold Brunner Prize for Distinguished Architecture in 1996 from the American Academy of Arts and Letters.

The work of the Studio reflects a broad range of interests. The firm has designed sets and costumes for a dance performance by the Elise Monte Dance Company with a score by Glenn Branca which premiered at Het Muziektheater in Amsterdam in 1990 and has its American premiere at the City Center Theater in New York City in 1991. A continuing collaboration with the Noguchi Museum resulted in the design of a show called 'Quiet Light' of Akari lamps and resin screens at the Takashimaya Gallery which traveled to museums in St. Louis and Montreal. A project entitled 'Domestic Arrangements: A Lab Report' was presented in a traveling exhibition which originated at the Walker Art Center, Minneapolis. An article by Paul Goldberger entitled, 'Rekindling the Fires of utopian Modernism', in reviewing this show, spoke of the effort to 'find within the Modernist vocabulary the same combination of social idealism and aesthetic discipline that motivated it (Utopian Modernism) in the 1920s.

Hereford College, a 525 student dormitory and dining facility at the University of Virginia, was completed in August of 1992. Paul Goldberger said '...It is only now, with the completion of a project by Tod Williams and Billie Tsien, that the University sees its first truly important post-Jefferson work, a residential college called New College. It is more different from Jefferson than anything that has been built in generations, but it rises to challenge him'. The Neurosciences Institute at The Scripps Research Institute Campus in La Jolla, California, a theoretical and laboratory research facility for the study of the brain, was completed last year. Herbert Muschamp of the *New York Times* called it 'a magnificent piece of work', and deemed it the best American building built in 1995.

Additional projects currently in the office include the Phoenix Art Museum and Theater, a new science building and a natatorium for the Emma Willard School, a natatorium and field house for the Cranbrook Schools in Michigan, the East Asian Studies Building at the University of California at Berkeley, and residences in New York City, Southampton, Millbrook, and Phoenix, Arizona.

Hariri & Hariri

Hariri & Hariri exemplifies the spirit of the emerging generation of architects. Gisue Hariri and Morjan Hariri, Iranian-born, Cornell educated sisters, opened their New York City practice in 1986. Dedicated to research and construction of innovative ideas, the firm's work has been acknowledged and recognized since its formation and has been exhibited in various galleries and architectural institutions. In August 1988 Charles Gandee featured Hariri & Hariri's work in *HG* magazine and wrote: '..no young New York firm signal's the dawn of the New architectural day more emphatically than Hariri & Hariri'. They are working, says another commentator, 'in a twenty-first-century, space age mode'.

Hariri & Hariri's work has been internationally published and awarded. Their comprehensive philosophy and work of the past ten years has been collected and featured in a book titled *Hariril & Hariril: Work in Progress* published by The Monacelli Press, in 1995. This book is organized around a number of important themes that have influenced the design and practice of the architects: politics and power; global culture; new technology; gender and identity; composition, construction, and materiality; paradoxical reality; and otherness.

Regarding architecture and contemporary culture, the Hariri's say: 'What is important in terms of cultural connections is the spirituality of Eastern thinking, which we are evaluating in the West, or rather from which we are evaluating the Western culture '.

Hariri & Hariri's work has been selected to be part of an exhibition at The Museum of Modern Art in New York City and Glasgow-1999 in the United Kingdom, in the summer of 1999, celebrating the beginning of a new millennium.

Marble Fairbanks Architects

Scott Marble and Karen Fairbanks began collaborating in 1990 and have worked on a wide range of residential, commercial, and institutional projects since that time. Prior to 1990, they were principals in separate firms and completed several small and large scale projects in and around New York City. They have been teaching at Columbia University since 1989, investigating themes and issues present in their built work.

Their office philosophy revolves around an extremely high quality of work on each project undertaken. All their projects are developed by both partners with a project architect and the MFA staff. The studio team follows the project from preliminary planning to completion.

Among their recent honors and awards, they were selected as Emerging Voices by the Architectural League of New York in 1998. In 1996, they were selected for 'Forty under Forty', an award recognizing the top forty designers and architects under the age of forty. The book *40 under 40* was published by Vitae Press and was released in early 1996. In 1997, 1996 and 1994, their work won Design Awards from the New York Chapter of the American Institute of Architects. In 1994, they were selected for a fellowship in Architecture from the New York Foundation for the Arts. Their work was selected by the Architectural League of New York for exhibition at the Urban Center in New York City as part of the Young Architects Forum in 1992. In 1991, they were selected as 1 of 5 finalists from over 600 offices worldwide in the Nara Convention Hall International Design Competition in Nara, Japan. This project has been exhibited throughout the world as part of their Preview Series in 1992-93. Their recent projects include the Louis and Jeanette Brooks Engineering Design Center for The Cooper Union, several private residences, Our Children's Foundation headquarters in Harlem, and new ticket booths and related entry elements for the Museum of Modern Art.

Karen Fairbanks

Karen Fairbanks is a partner at Scott Marble & Karen Fairbanks Architects. Prior to establishing the partnership she was a designer at Cooper Robertson and Partners, Davis, Brody & Associates, and Graham Gund Associates.

She received her Master of Architecture degree at Columbia University where she won the AIA Medal in 1987, the William Kinne Fellowship in 1987, the Fred L Liebman Book Award in 1986, and was the representative for Columbia University in the SOM Traveling Scholarship Competition in 1986. She received her Bachelor of Science in Architecture degree from the University of Michigan in 1981.

Karen Fairbanks is currently the Director of the Barnard and Columbia Colleges Architecture Program, and is a full time faculty member of Barnard College and has been teaching at Columbia University since 1989. She has also taught at Parsons School of Design and Rensselaer Polytechnic Institute. She was a New York Foundation for the Arts, Fellow in Architecture in 1988 and 1994. She has served as a panelist for the Architecture Awards for the New York Foundation for the Arts and on the Young Architects Committee for the Architectural League of New York.

Scott Marble

Prior to establishing the partnership he was a partner in Russ Drinker & Scott Marble Architects and a designer at Bausman & Gill Associates, Aedificare Architects, Peter L. Gluck & Partners, and Shepherd & Boyd USA.

He received his Master of Architecture degree from Columbia University in 1986 where he was awarded the AIA Award and the William Kinne Fellowship for his proposal The Architecture of the Algerian Sahara. He received his Bachelor of Environmental Design degree from Texas A & M University in 1983.

Scott has taught at Columbia University Graduate School of Architecture, Planning, and Preservation since 1987, serving as the Co-ordinator of Graduate Studios from 1992-4. He has been the editor of *Abstract*, the catalog of the Graduate School of Architecture, Planning and Preservation of Columbia University, since 1995. In 1987 he co-edited the book *Architecture and Body*, published by Rizzoli. Scott was a New York Foundation for the Arts, Fellow in Architecture in 1994. In 1992 he was winner in the Young Architects Forum sponsored by the Architectural League of New York and served on the selection committee in 1993.

Scott Marble & Karen Fairbanks Architects form a collaborative architecture studio working on both built work and speculative projects. International competitions form a significant part of our work as we attempt to converge the ideas and interests pursued in these typically larger public buildings with those of our smaller scale built work.

Although different projects facilitate different degrees of conceptual investigation, we understand all of our work in a social and cultural context that conditions the specifics of each project. We have most recently been investigating the potential of architecture to embrace both the space of a global network and the more specific space of a given site, program(s), and time. While acknowledging the emergence of a linked world culture, we work with the premise that societies and cultures, at the turn of the millennium, are (still) heterogeneous entities with instances of unique and distinctive characteristics which architecture can and should embody. To attempt to erase these distinctions limits the possibility of revealing the most potent and active critical tendencies of society – those existing and already within. Interpretations and elaborations of the cultural and programmatic, as well as physical, contexts surrounding an architectural project play an instrumental role in how we conceive of our work. Consequently, we have begun to think about architecture as intervention that absorbs and reconfigures rather than confronts context. Much of our work deals with spatial organisations which encourage multiple patterns of use acknowledging the constructive dynamic between the context and the architectural intervention. Rather than formalizing specific spatial and programmatic relationships, our design methodology focuses on architecture as a strategy to establish conditions for these relationships to occur. The architectural intervention reframes the existing context and potentially reprograms public use provoking new forms of social exchange.

Kolatan / MacDonald Studio

Kolatan / Mac Donald Studio was founded by Sulan Kolatan and William Mac Donald in 1988. The firm has recently been awarded the 44th Annual Progressive Architecture Citation Award, the 'Forty under Forty' Award, the Emerging Voices Award, the Fifth Young Architects Award, and the New York Foundation for the Arts Grant and Fellowship.

The work of Kolatan / Mac Donald Studio is in the permanent collections of the Museum of Modern Art in New York, the San Francisco Museum of Modern Art, and the Avery Library Collection. In addition, their projects have been widely exhibited; some of the more recent venues have been; the Deutsches Architektur Museum in Frankfurt, Germany; Columbia University; the Architectural Association in London, England, and the Sandra Gering Gallery in New York City. Their recent work has been featured internationally in the following publications; the *New York Times*, the *Village Voice*, the *Wall Street Journal* (newspapers), *Architecture Magazine*, *Architectural Design Magazine* (AD), *Lotus International*, *Architecture and Urbanism* (A+U), *Global Architecture* (GA), *Oculus*, "D", 'A3', L' Arca, and *Flash Art International*.

Sulan Kolatan

Born in Istanbul, Turkey. Kolatan received a Diplom Ingenieur degree from Rheinisch-Westfalische Technische Hochschule Aachen, Germany, and a Master of Science in Architecture and Building Design from Columbia University. She divided her time equally between Istanbul, and Cologne until 1982. After having finished her graduate studies at Columbia, she settled in New York City. In addition to their practice, she has taught architecture as a Visiting Professor at Barnard College, Ohio State University, the University of Pennsylvania, the Institute for Advanced Architectural Studies in Basel, Switzerland and in Venice, Italy. Since 1990, she has been teaching at Columbia University's Graduate School of Architecture, Planning, and Preservation.

William J. MacDonald

Born in Milford, Massachusetts, USA, MacDonald studied at the Architectural Association in London, England and received a Bachelor of Architecture from Syracuse University before obtaining a Master of Science in Architecture and Urban Design from Columbia University. His previous teaching experience was at the University of Virginia, and as a Visiting Professor at Ohio State University, the University of Pennsylvania, the Institute for Advanced Architectural Studies in Venice, Italy. In addition to their practice, he has taught at Columbia University's Graduate School of Architecture, Planning, and Preservation since 1985.

George Ranalli

George Ranalli was born in New York City in 1946. He received his A.Arch. from Pratt Institute in 1972 and M.Arch. from the Graduate School of Design at Harvard University in 1974. Since 1976 he has been a professor of Architectural Design at Yale University, and fro 1988 to 1989 he was the William Henry Bishop Chaired Professor in Architectural Design. His work has been exhibited at the Cooper-Hewitt mMuseum; Sperone-Westwater Gallery: Museum of Contemporary Art, Chicago; Museum of Finnish Architecture, Finland; Centre Pompidou, France; Deutsches Architekturmuseum, Frankfurt, Germany; the Xvii Triennale Di Milano, Italy. The Valentine Chair # 2 has been taken into the permanent collection of 20th Century Art and Design at The Metropolitan Museum of Art, New York in September 1992. In 1988 he was awarded a New York Foundation for the Arts Grant with an artist fellowship in Architecture. The Dentsu Co. of Tokyo commissioned a project for Japan in 1989-90 called K-project. The Union Co. of Osaka is now producing a line of architectural hardware for commercial international production. This hardware is now in the permanent collection of 20th Century Architecture and Design at the Denver Art Museum. His architectural and design work has been published internationally in such journals as *Domus*, *A & U*, *Progressive Architecture*, *L'Architettura*, *G. A. Houses*, *Architectural Digest*, *Architecture D'Aujourd'hui*, *Architectural Design* and *Lotus*. A monograph of his work entitled *George Ranalli: Buildings and Projects* is published by Princeton Architectural Press, New York City. The August issue of *A&U (Architecture and Urbanism)*, 1990 has a special feature of his work. A new monograph in the series CASAS, entitled *George Ranalli: Architect*, is just published.

The *Sunday New York Times* Arts and Leisure Section on March 6, 1994 featured a review of his project for the Fashion Center Building. The Fashion Center Building Project was awarded an American Institute of Architects New York Chapter Architecture Award for 1994. The office was awarded an American Institute of Architecture New York Chapter Design Award in the 1995 Design Awards Program for the project Pool & Pool House for 'C' Family and also awarded an American Institute of Architects New York Chapter Design Award in the 1996 Design Awards Program for the project Indoor Low Pool Buildings. In the 1997 Design Awards Program of the American Institute of Architects New York Chapter, Mr Ranalli was awarded a Projects Award for the Stonington Historical Society, Library/Archive Building in Stonington, Connecticut.

Mr Ranalli designed the show 'Frank Lloyd Wright: Designs for an American Landscape', 1922-1932 for the Whitney Museum in 1997, and was awarded the commission to design the installation for the exhibit of the work of Carlo Scarpa, scheduled for 1999 at the Canadian Center for Architecture in Montreal, Canada. He has been invited to lecture on his work in many schools of architecture, museums, and art organizations in all parts of the world. Mr Ranalli is currently working on a house addition in Bedford, New York, a design for a renovation and addition to the Student Union Building at Queens College in New York, and a 3,500 square foot commercial building for Yale University.

Author's Note

Ivor Richards is both an architect and an academic teacher of architecture, and is a Member of the Royal Institute of British Architects. In practice during the 1970s and 1980s he collaborated with Sir Leslie Martin in his Cambridge studio. The major buildings that resulted from this collaboration include the Centre for Contemporary Art for the Gulbenkian Foundation in Lisbon, Portugal (1983); the Royal Scottish Academy of Music and Drama, Glasgow (1988); and the Faculty of Music for the University of Cambridge (1978-84). Richards' independent architectural practice has also included a series of Courtyard Houses and an Ecumenical Church, all in the Cambridge area. This work has been widely published and two courthouses received RIBA awards. The church was exhibited in the Venice Biennale collection 'Sacred Space in the Modern Age' in 1992. His collected works have been exhibited in both the USA and the UK, including a 30-year retrospective in 1998, entitled 'LINKAGES: architecture, ideas and education'.

Richards has written extensively on the American master Richard Meier, and on a series of other contemporary architects across the world who have extended the modern tradition in architecture.

Ivor Richards has taught continuously since 1986, both in the UK and the USA. He was Professor of Architectural Design at the University of Cardiff, Wales between 1986-94, and is currently Professor of Architecture at the University of Newcastle, UK.

In the USA, Richards has taught at the University of Houston and at Texas A&M University. He was awarded the Hyde Chair for Excellence in Architecture at the University of Nebraska, Lincoln, in the fall semester 1991. He has been continuously affiliated with New York and its architects since 1993, as a result of his research and study of the work of Richard Meier, the subject of a major forthcoming publication.

Manhattan Lofts is a further product of his connection with New York City, and its architectural production.